Enjoy
prey -

2-14-24

Seth

Seth

by **Eric Deters**

Acclaim Press™
MORLEY, MISSOURI

Bulldog Media, Inc.
5247 Madison Pike
Independence, KY 41051

Distributed by:

Acclaim Press
— Your Next Great Book —

P.O. Box 238
Morley, MO 63767
(573) 472-9800
www.acclaimpress.com

ISBN: 978-1-956027-39-6 | 1-956027-39-4
Library of Congress Control Number: 2022947138

First Printing: 2022
Printed in the United States of America
10 9 8 7 6 5 4 3 2 1

This publication was produced using available information.
The publisher regrets it cannot assume responsibility for errors or omissions.

Contents

DEDICATION

This book is dedicated to my brother, Seth, and to those who live every day with special needs. May God bless, strengthen, and comfort them.

I also dedicate this book to the loving, patient, and courageous parents and caregivers of those living with special needs who wake up each morning to face challenges the rest of us may never face while receiving blessings the rest of us may never fully experience.

PREFACE

Even the most casual student of the Christian Bible recalls the tragic story of Cain and Abel, the two sons of Adam and Eve. The story is told in *Genesis*, the first chapter of the Old Testament. Cain murdered Abel in a jealous rage. God then cursed Cain with a mark upon his body for everyone to see as he roamed the earth throughout his remaining years.

I suspect fewer students of the Christian Bible know about the third son of Adam and Eve. When Eve gave birth to her third son, she proclaimed, "God has given me another child. He will take the place of Abel, who was killed by Cain." Eve named her third son Seth. Seth is from the Hebrew word meaning "to give."

God bestowed upon my family the gift of our own Seth. To the members of my family, Seth is not the third son of Adam and Eve but is our son and brother. He is the seventh child and the fourth son of our parents, Charles and Mary Sue Deters. Seth is a brother to ten and a friend of an entire community.

This book is Seth's remarkable story which chronicles his influence on our family and the many other lives he has touched.

INTRODUCTION

I began writing this book years ago but never finished it. Consequently, Seth's story is long overdue for publication. I promised Seth I would write his story and have it published. I kept that promise because I would never want to let him down.

PROLOGUE

Every day for many years, Mary Sue Deters left the comfort of her house, stepped out the front door, and embarked upon a three-mile walk up and back to the end of Green Road. She completed this self-imposed exercise routine to battle her late-in-life diagnosis of diabetes. In her eighties at the time, Mary Sue Deters completed her daily journey regardless of the weather. As she walked along the side of the long country road, she thought, prayed, and reflected. She carried a wooden staff in her hand as if she were Moses leading his people from Egypt. This walk is not a flat course but is full of rolling hills and grassy and wooded landscapes past neighboring farms. The discipline of this daily exercise, along with daily Mass, kept Mary Sue mentally, physically, and spiritually fit. Now ninety-three, she no longer takes this walk. However, she remains our family's spiritual rock.

Every morning for decades, Seth Riley Deters awoke at 6:00 a.m. without the assistance of an alarm clock. He followed this routine, without exception, three hundred and sixty-five days a year. Seth dressed, stumbled out the same door, and walked toward a golf cart parked outside the house. Seth is now fifty-eight years old, one year younger than me. His routine remains the same to this day. Seth's internal wake-up call allows him to perform his daily chore of feeding grain to the horses in their stalls before the other farmhands arrive to turn them out to the grass-filled paddocks surrounding the horse barns. The horses on the farm depend on Seth for breakfast. He never lets them down.

Anyone who works hard deserves admiration. But Seth's work deserves special accolades because he has been afflicted with, and lived with, cerebral palsy since the earliest days of his life. While my mother is our family's spiritual rock, Seth is our family's soul. Although quite different in nature and purpose, the daily walks once taken by Mary Sue Deters and Seth Deters bound them together on a journey that began many years ago.

SETH

At fifty-eight years old, Seth is no taller than five feet three inches. His hairline is vanquished. He possesses only a rim of brown hair that circles above his ears. He always wears a baseball cap to conceal his baldness. His lack of hair is a point of vanity and troubles him more than it should. Despite daily brushing, Seth's teeth are stained yellow. Although he once avoided dentist visits, Seth now regularly shows up for his dental appointments. However, sometimes Seth is moody. When he's in a serious mood, he not only broods but can also lash out in anger. In between these two extreme moods, he carries a melancholy of calm.

Seth has a cut jawline and strong chin from having no extra "meat on his bones." His full lips bear a permanent scar from one of his more severe falls, which took a chunk out of his lip.

The back of Seth's head, as well as other parts of his body, reveal scars obtained long ago from frequent falls against brick, concrete, and blacktop. He walks with a broken gait which causes him to rock side to side after each step, similar to Redd Foxx when he played Fred Sanford on *Sanford and Son*. Although it appears Seth could fall over anytime, he usually manages to maintain his balance. Seth has strong hands with rugged knuckles and calloused palms from years of wielding a broomstick and pitchfork while working on the farm. The muscles in his arms and legs are taut and strong. When he weighed only one hundred and twenty pounds, Seth's abdominal muscles formed a "six-pack" from all his walking. While he's still trim,

Seth is now heavier from age and his current use of the golf cart he drives around the farm.

When Seth talks, he speaks with a slightly broken voice like Tarzan in the old movies featuring Johnny Weissmuller. Although his sentences are fragmented, he speaks clearly and is easily understood. Seth also speaks with simplicity. Adjectives and adverbs are absent from his vocabulary. A typical drawled statement would be: "Dad-dy. You take me game".

Our older sister, Suzy, recalls special moments she witnessed between Seth and Grandma Deters. Suzy remembers Grandma Deters would always get down on the floor and play with Seth when he was a toddler. Blocks were a favorite of theirs. Whenever Grandma Deters came to visit, she always brought Seth something special.

Over the years, Seth earned several nicknames from family and friends. Many stuck, and several remain with him today. Seth was always a happy child. Since his middle name is Riley, somewhere along the line, he earned the nickname Smiley Riley. In the family archives, we have a home movie epitomizing Smiley Riley. A young Seth and his younger brother, Richard, are seen splashing water in a small shallow plastic pool to their hearts' content. Seth is smiling without a care in the world.

As a youngster, I suffered from a speech impediment and could not pronounce many words. In a creative fashion, I made up my own words and created my own language. I was often teased about my linguistic creativity. The ones I still remember are "yehyeh" for ghost, "keealum" for bulldozers, and "Peppie" for Seth. There was no rhyme or reason for any of them. However, Peppie stuck for a long time. Seth became my little brother, Peppie.

A farm worker, Jimmy Noland, gave Seth another nickname that still endures. One day, Seth wore one of those classic Elmer Fudd hunter's hats. When Jimmy started calling him Elmer Fudd, Seth became Elmer forevermore.

Seth is a character. He may be afflicted with cerebral palsy, but he has an engaging personality and idiosyncrasies that are endearing. Seth can be a real charmer, especially with the ladies. Seth develops a crush on many women and younger ladies. Despite his denial, I tease him about his crush on my wife, Mary. Seth frequently requested that Mary take him shopping when he needed something. Mary also took him to his weekly bowling matches. When I would show up in lieu of Mary, his first question always was, "Where is Mary?" Seth could not hide his disappointment when I was his driver.

Being a character is actually a family trait extending through known family history. Seth is not a character by accident. The first Deters in our family to touch American soil was Heinrich Clemons. He came to the United States in 1848 from Oldenburg, Germany. Oldenburg is located in Lower Saxony in northwest Germany. There was a Catholic Bishop in Oldenburg with the last name Deters. The reason for Heinrich Clemons Deters transatlantic continental voyage was to avoid the turmoil of the German civil wars going on at that time. All of Germany was divided into numerous principalities that warred against each other and the efforts to unite them. I suspect Heinrich may have been a draft dodger.

The Germans who fled Germany in 1848 were called the Forty-Eighters. Henry Villard was a political refugee along with Heinrich Clemons Deters. Villard was a Civil War correspondent and later founded the AP. He won and lost fortunes many times over. Villard was also a partner with Thomas Edison in founding General Electric.

Heinrich set up a saloon across from the City Hall in Cincinnati on Plum Street. The building still stands today. Heinrich became part of the German American community, which dominated Cincinnati's population and the entire state of Ohio. By the early 1900s, the population of Cincinnati was more than 60% German American. Fondly called "Zinzinnati" by its German residents, Cincinnati was home to brewing companies like Christian Moerlein, numerous German language printers and newspapers, and German-speaking schools. The evidence of the German migration was everywhere, from the brick and stone Bavarian architecture to the names of canals and neighborhoods like Cincinnati's Over the Rhine.

In late 1917, the waves of the anti-German movement fueled by World War I began to hit Cincinnati. The Germans of Cincinnati scrambled to hide their heritage out of fear of persecution. German language printings became obsolete. German schools began to close. Saloons even took pretzels off their counter as every bit of German heritage was eradicated from the city. Restaurants began to sell "liberty slaw" instead of sauerkraut. Doctors diagnosed "liberty measles" instead of German measles. As the Great War advanced, so did the anti-German movement. Germans found themselves unemployed, beaten, and even lynched on several occasions.

Heinrich Clemons had four sons. Charles Sabbath, one of Heinrich's sons, was my great grandfather. Charles Sabbath died young. A drinker, he succumbed to liver sclerosis. I named my first daughter after his wife, Caroline. Charles and Caroline were blessed with four sons, Clemons Bernard, Charles, Paul, and Frank. Clemons Bernard was my grandfather.

The oldest, Charles, owned a store he appropriately named Deters and Daughters. Married late in life, he had five daughters and no sons. Charles was a butcher. He owned a butcher shop, liquor store, and grocery store, all under one roof. He and his wife, Jan, lived over the store. Uncle Charlie had a great saying, "Three things you need to remember, one, if you think nickels, you make nickels; you'll never be rich working for somebody else; and if you've got the money, you can hire the accountant for the details." Not bad advice. Uncle Charlie lived past eighty despite enjoying a good drink and a steady diet of red meat and chain-smoking cigarettes since he was a kid. Charlie was the real-world tough guy of the four brothers. He believed America should have bombed Iran and taken their oil amid the Iranian Hostage Crisis.

Uncle Charlie's five daughters are each "characters" in their own right; tough and opinionated in true Deters fashion. They are certainly not shrinking violets. Charlotte is a great example.

She wears leather and is a biker. No helmet dons her head as she races down the road on her chopper. In candor, I'm a tough guy, but I think Charlotte could kick my ass. Charlotte manages restaurants. Rosie is an accountant. Denise is a registered nurse. Pauline runs the family store with her younger sister, Jennifer. I had the honor of being the server for all their weddings.

Uncle Paul lived in Evansville, Indiana, and founded a jewelry store he named *Deters Jewelers*. Paul's son, P.R., and his wife operated the jewelry store until they retired. P.R. was fun and handled the family's jewelry needs when he ran the store. Paul was a dapper golfer. Sales suited his fun-loving personality.

Frank, the youngest brother, passed away last. I have no idea what Frank did for a living if anything. He is survived by Aunt Claire, a tall, smart, red-headed Texan.

My grandfather, Clemens "Bud" Deters, worked as the editor of the *Kentucky Times Star*. When the Scripps Howard Company bought the paper in 1958, he lost his job via a Western Union telegram. My Uncle Jim kept the telegram is in the Deters "Museum". After losing his job, Grandpa made his living in real estate and insurance. My grandfather was the Chairman of the Northern Kentucky Greater Cincinnati Airport Board when he died at 84. He was on the Board for over twenty years. I had lunch with Grandpa Deters every week, and I miss him to this day.

Bud and his wife, Grandma Cedora, met as teenagers. Grandpa was riding a bike, and Grandma caused him to wreck. According to family legend, Grandpa berated Grandma over the incident. However, Grandpa changed his mind about Grandma and soon began courting her. Apparently, Grandma's father didn't care much for my grandpa at first. It's funny to think of my grandpa being a concern to a father of a young girl. Only eighteen years old, they ran off and eloped. They were married for over sixty years and had five children: Jerry, Charlie, Joan, Jim, and Kathy. Charlie is my father.

My Grandpa was a kind and gentle man. He cared about his family and community above all else. Grandma was a stay-at-home mom who cooked breakfast, lunch, and dinner for my grandpa. I didn't know until her later years that she smoked cigarettes. She never smoked in front of us. Grandma snuck cigarettes like a teenager. Despite the unhealthy habit, Grandma Deters lived past ninety.

My grandfather, my father, and my father's brother, Jerry, started building homes when Jerry was only seventeen and my father was only fifteen. The first house they built stood on Senour Road in Independence, Kentucky. The house still stands today. From there, they started building subdivisions in the town of Taylor Mill. Later, they bought land in Lakeside Park and built the Lakeside Park Subdivision. All these locations are in the area known as Northern Kentucky, across the Ohio River from Cincinnati.

When they first purchased the Lakeside property, my grandfather couldn't believe how much they paid per acre for the land, stating it would never work. Later, my Uncle Jerry lived in West Lakeside, where he raised his family. My father almost bought a house there before buying property on Green Road in rural Kenton County. After being in the home building business for a while, my Uncle Jerry built the Drawbridge Motor Inn in 1970. At that point, he quit building houses. Jerry was also one of the founders of the Northern Kentucky Home Builders Association. My father decided to practice law because he was tired of digging ditches.

My mother, Mary Sue, was born in Harlan County, Kentucky. Her family went to the Methodist Church in Harlan. My mother attended the Methodist Sunday School. The church only had mass on the first Sunday of the month. So, my mother attended mass on that designated Sunday and went to the Methodist Sunday School the rest of the time.

My mother attended Harlan County High School. Their mascot was the Green Dragons. I took a political trip to Harlan County with my mother in 1991. While we were there, I purchased a hat with the school's name. I still have it. It's a good luck charm. I always wore it when I played flag football. I also gave my only son the middle name Harlan so he would know his mountain roots.

My mother graduated from Harlan High in 1948. Having little money, she never received a copy of her senior picture. Years ago, I blew up her photo in the yearbook so she would have a senior picture like my dad and all of us kids to hang on the wall in her home.

When my mother left Harlan County, Father Henry Hanses arranged for her to stay at Mount St. Martins while she attended Villa Madonna College. At that time, Mount St. Martins was a home for working girls and students. Mount St. Martins was formerly a convent and later became an old folk's home. Mount St. Martins is no longer in existence. The site is now a K-Mart in the Newport Shopping Center. When Mom lived at Mount St. Martins, there was nothing behind it where the shopping center is now, so she and her friends would go out and take sun baths and play ball out there.

My parents met at the end of my mother's freshman year at Mount St. Martins in the spring of 1949. My mother and father both attended Villa Madonna College. Although they were the same age, my father was two years ahead of my mother because he had gone to Latin school. Mom majored in English and Art at Villa Madonna College. In 1968, Villa Madonna College was re-named Thomas More College after the patron saint of lawyers. Today, Thomas More University remains a private, Catholic, small liberal arts college in Northern Kentucky.

My maternal grandmother's name was Lucy. Her maiden name was Patterson. Lucy's family hailed from Arkansas. I once handled a case in front of an Arkansas federal judge named Patterson by marriage. By the time we finished speaking, we had thought we were related. Lucy was proudly a "snuggin", which is Arkansas "white trash." After finding her way to Appalachia in Harlan County, Lucy attended and received a teaching degree from Alice Lloyd College in Knox County, Kentucky. Lucy then married my grandfather, Albert Krippenstapel. She was a teacher in the Harlan Public Schools. Lucy also taught at Kits, a coal camp.

Albert Krippenstapel, my maternal grandfather, was the typesetter for the *Harlan Daily Enterprise,* the local newspaper. My mother recalls his type machine faced the window of an alley in downtown Harlan. When she returned home from school, she would turn into that alley and knock on the window. When he saw her, he'd say, "Hey, Toots." Grandpa Albert always called her Toots. When she walked in, he'd hand her a nickel so she could buy a candy bar.

My mother was only fourteen when her father died. Grandpa Albert had strep throat, which turned into Bright's Disease, a kidney ailment. Since there was no dialysis at the time, he was forced into an infirmary in Louisville, Kentucky. At that time, Grandpa Albert was told he probably had about six months to live. He came back home and lived for two years after that, but my mother recalls him being extremely sick during the last year of his life. On the day of his funeral, the movie, *Little Women,* was showing in movie theatres. It was the first one, with Katherine Hepburn. My mother wanted to see the movie but figured she wouldn't get to go. Much to her surprise, her mother allowed her to see the movie with her little sister, Lucy Ellen. Lucy Ellen was only three at the time. When the two were walking home after the movie, Lucy Ellen looked up at my mother and asked where their Daddy was. Mom told Lucy Ellen he was in heaven. Whenever I think of my fourteen-year-old mother losing her father, it breaks my heart.

When my parents were married, Lucy and my mother's younger sister, Lucy Ellen, moved to Covington, Kentucky. We called Lucy, Granny. To this day, I've never met anyone in Northern Kentucky who calls their grandmother Granny. I loved Granny. Our Granny was special. I suppose you must be pretty special to be a Granny. She always reminded me of Granny on the *Beverly Hillbillies.* She looked just like her. But our Granny never chased anyone with a shotgun, as far as we know.

After moving to Covington, Granny taught first grade at the Fourth District School. She and Lucy Ellen lived in an apartment across from the school. Lucy Ellen attended Notre Dame Academy in Covington and then the University of Kentucky. Lucy Ellen did student teaching at Highlands High School in Ft. Thomas, Kentucky, and Holmes High School in Covington, where she taught literature and English. She's our family's top scholar and is quite cosmopolitan. Lucy Ellen lived in Manhattan for two years and taught at a high school on Long Island. She's written several books and is now a retired professor from Clemson University.

As kids, when we went to Granny's apartment, she always gave us treats of Wrigley chewing gum, M&M's, and ice cream with Hershey syrup. She always fixed me my favorite meal, a bowl of baked beans with brown sugar. Granny also made the best peanut butter and jelly sandwiches, making sure to spread everything to the edge of the bread.

Granny always watched us when our parents went out for an evening or if they went out of town. When Granny watched us, she liked to have fun. Granny enjoyed irritating our mother with her laxed rules. As kids, she would tell us off-color jokes. For example, she would hold a deck of cards behind her and drop them slowly as if to make the sound of a cow doing its' business. She never told dirty jokes, just a little left of clean. Whenever a new Disney movie came out, she took us to the Madison Theatre in Covington to see the matinee. I remember it like it was yesterday. My favorite was *Bedknobs and Broomsticks*. Granny also took us to the five-and-dime store, Walgreens. Granny religiously watched daytime soap operas. She referred to them as her shows.

Granny always came to our house at Christmas and on all special occasions. She developed the strangest relationship with the gander, the male goose, which lived on our farm lake. The gander was mean as hell. He would come up to the house, a couple hundred yards from the lake, chase us and snap at us. He became a regular attack gander. He also did his business all over the driveway. There's a reason the word "goose" is used to describe a loose stool. When Granny came out of the house, she would cackle, and the darn gander would cackle back and come running up to the house. It was the darndest thing to witness. If any of us got near Granny, he would bite the heck out of us. Knowing she was there, he would walk around the house and peck on the windows, calling for her. It was a bizarre "love affair" between Granny and the gander.

When we were teenagers, we could always count on Granny for advice. She always told my sisters to make sure the boys "kept that thing in their pants." When I started to drive, I began taking Granny to lunch once a month to her favorite restaurant, Bonanza. I always looked forward to my lunches with Granny.

During my freshman year in law school, I came home one day to horrible news. Granny had been killed in a pedestrian car accident. At eighty-four, Granny was very active. She would walk from her apartment to the stores in Covington. As she received the walk sign, a van turned right into the crosswalk, killing her. My parents and my sister, Suzy, went to the hospital to identify her. I couldn't believe it. Granny was the closest person I ever knew who died.

One photograph sums up Granny in our memory. At over eighty years old, she climbed on the back of my brother Jed's dirt bike to take a ride. Granny didn't wear a helmet. The picture shows her big smile and her sense of fun and adventure. Granny rarely went to church, but she read the bible every day. On the day she died, her bible was opened, and the chapter and verse which read "Thou knows not the day and hour of your death" was highlighted.

My parents married in 1956 after my father finished law school at the University of Cincinnati. As Mom recalls, she and Dad dated a little bit, and then he went to Germany for two years. When Dad returned, he practiced law for a year, and then they married. When my parents went on their honeymoon to Gatlinburg, Tennessee, their friends, the Dressmans and Dunns, went with them. Maybe this was common at the time but certainly is not common today. Legend has it that Jim Dressman and William Dunn, two future judges, did a fertility dance on my parents' honeymoon bed. I suppose it worked since my mother bore my father eleven children in sixteen years. Jim Dressman topped my dad. He had twelve children. I have no idea if a fertility dance was performed on his honeymoon bed.

My oldest sister, Amy, is very religious, like our mother. Amy Marie was named for Mother Mary and our Aunt Marie. According to Mom, Amy was very tiny at birth. She was full term but only weighed four pounds and three ounces. Now Amy lives up the road on the family farm. I don't believe she's a traditional oldest child. Amy is not as assertive as the rest of us.

The second oldest is Suzy. Suzy was named Suzanne simply because my mother liked the name. Mom couldn't think of a suitable middle name, so Suzy went without one. Suzy later took Maureen as her confirmation name. Suzy's nickname growing up was "Boss." She still is a boss, strong and opinionated.

Thad is the oldest boy. Thad Patterson was named for St. Jude, and Granny's maiden name which was Patterson. Thad is the oldest boy stereotype in that none of us would ever mess with him. He's strong and tough. Thad is also the only real farmer in the family. In my opinion, he's also the most intelligent. Ironic because Thad never graduated from college. Regardless, he was the only one of us who ever earned an A in math and science. Thad is a retired railroad engineer.

Jed Kerstan was named for Jedediah, meaning beloved by God. Kerstan was a variation of the word Christian. My mother pointed out that Jed was not named for Jed Clampett of the *Beverly Hillbillies* from that era. However, she laughed as she said he took on the entire Jed Clampett persona. Jed was the most mechanical and conservative of the children. He rehabbed tractors. As a lawyer, he performed real estate and bank work. Jed tragically died of metastatic kidney cancer in 2015, at the age of fifty-four.

Sara was named Sara Lisa because my mom liked the name. Sara is the organizer of family events. For years, her nickname was "Mouse" because she was so tiny. However, she eventually became known as "Boss", just like Suzy.

Like Sara, I was named Eric because my parents liked the name. My middle name is Charles for my dad. Eric means king. Charles means strong. I like that. I'm the middle child, number six of eleven. Like most middle children, I'm socially adaptable to all age groups. But I'm also the "black sheep" of the family.

Seth came after me. Seth Riley is named after the third son of Adam and Eve. His middle name is Riley for Grandma Deters.

Next came Celia Jane. Mother thought Celia was a beautiful name from the time she was a young girl back in Harlan. The man who played the organ at the Methodist church in Harlan had a daughter named Celia. According to my mother, this was a beautiful child with blue eyes and blond hair they kept perfectly groomed. The organist's daughter always wore little white gloves to Sunday School and was always well-behaved. My mother recalls that when Celia finished playing with something, she put it away before she played with something else. According to Mom, she and Dad both liked the name Jane Frances. But they named her Celia Jane partly because of the organist's daughter. Mom laughs because our Celia is nothing like that Celia. Our Celia is a "tomboy." She once trained horses. Celia also ate the paint off her crib and the windowsills. She chewed on wood. Despite my mother's best efforts, Celia chewed on and ate everything she could get in her mouth.

Richard is named after Bishop Richard Ackerman and Father Henry Hanses. Father Henry Hanses was the pastor at St. John's Church in Covington, Kentucky. He baptized all eleven of us. A true Saint of a human being, Father Hanses worked with the Appalachian poor and cared for everyone inside or outside of his inner-city parish. My mother believes Richard should have been a priest. Richard is the boy equivalent to

Amy. He's also a lawyer and is the quietest in the family. Yet, Richard was also a Sergeant in the Marine Corps Reserves.

Nathan Blaze was named for a devotion to St. Blaze. In the Catholic Church, once a year, all Catholics have their throats blessed by the priest in a blessing of St. Blaze. My mother was amused as she pointed out that Nathan had more sore throats than any of the other children. Nathan is quiet. However, he's the Playboy in the family. At age forty-nine, he's still single.

Jeremy John is the youngest. According to my mother, his name originates from my father's doodling. Dad heard the name John Jeremiah and loved it. He always doodled the name John Jeremiah and claimed he would use John Jeremiah Sims as his pen name if he ever wrote a book. My parents compromised and named him Jeremy John to be a little more contemporary. Jeremy is the classic youngest child. He's the most spoiled of our clan.

~

I marvel at politicians stressing "family values" in their political propaganda. I believe every family has its own uniqueness and values, no matter its size or social circumstances. Family values vary. Common threads run through families. But if you showed up in the home of any American family on Thanksgiving, Christmas morning or for a summer barbeque, you would witness that family's unique fabric, traditions, and structure. I love how each family feels special and unique. I think that's the way it should be because each family is special and unique.

Over the years, I've enjoyed listening to my parents tell the special and unique stories that make up our family history. My mother talks about the little house on Grace Avenue in Latonia, Kentucky, where she and my father lived when they were first married. After Amy was born in 1957, they moved to Ashland Avenue in Latonia. Latonia is a southern section of Covington. It is a residential neighborhood with a large commercial center. Our Ashland Avenue home was the first house on the right, past the public playground. A brick wall separated the ball fields from the house. As youngsters, we thought the wall was as tall as the Great Wall of China. The three-foot wall still stands today.

Mom told me the story about Chris Baxter, a nurse's aide in the obstetrical department at Saint Elizabeth Hospital. According to Mom, Chris Baxter loved the babies she worked with at the hospital and saw them all as individuals with different personalities. Mom claimed Chris Baxter fell in love with Amy. When Mom returned to Saint Elizabeth Hospital the next year to have my sister, Suzy, Chris Baxter asked about Amy. That conversation sparked an ongoing relationship between Chris Baxter, my parents, and their children. Chris Baxter stayed with Amy and Suzy while my mother was in the hospital having Thad. She also stayed to help when my mother came home. From that time on, Dad would call Chris Baxter whenever Mom had a baby. She would take care of the children while Mom was in the hospital and stay for a while to help after Mom and the new baby came home.

According to my mom, Amy and Suzy were a big help with the younger children as we came along. They gave us baths at night. Sara helped a bit with Seth but was more helpful with Nathan and Jeremy because she was a little older by the time they arrived.

Although my parents had a large family of their own, they also opened our home to others in need. According to Mom, Monsignor John Murphy told her and my dad about a young girl who needed a home. My Mom was pregnant with my brother, Jed, at the time. This girl had been adopted by a wealthy couple. The couple had brought her up with a lavish lifestyle and expensive designer clothes. The girl was beautiful with Hispanic traits. As time went on, the wife became jealous of her. The couple decided they didn't want her anymore and brought her back. Consequently, Monsignor Murphy asked my parents to take her into our home.

This young girl came and lived with our family for a few years. My parents sent her to Notre Dame Academy. However, she chose not to stay and graduate. When she turned sixteen, she decided to go back to her biological mother in California. Looking back, my mother feels that taking this girl in may not have been the best idea. My father thought she could be a big help to my mother. He worked long hours and was never home except at night. But Mom feels she and my father were too young to make it a good situation for all involved.

My father enjoys telling the story of my sister Sara's unexpected entrance into this world on November 2, 1961. Sara is my parents' fifth child and their third daughter. They regard Sara's birth as one of the most dramatic and exciting events that occurred while the family lived at the Ashland Avenue house.

As my dad recounts the story, he was at his office that afternoon when Mom called to tell him she thought the baby was coming. He said her voice was weak. My Grandpa, Bud Deters, was in Dad's office at the time. The office was at Third and Garrard Street. Dad asked Grandpa to watch the other kids while he took Mom to the hospital. Dad arrived at the house before Grandpa. When he came in the door, Mom was back in the bedroom. Amy was with her. The rest of the children were playing. Suzy was three. Thad was two. Jed was one.

Dad ran into the bedroom. Mom told him she thought it was too late to go to the hospital because the baby was coming. So, Dad looked and could see the baby's head.

Dad ran to the house next door. He rang the doorbell but didn't wait for our neighbor to answer. He jumped over the porch railing and went to the next house because he knew Margaret Sharkey, the woman who lived there, was a nurse and the daughter of a physician. Dad went to school with her son, Tom, who was also a doctor.

According to Dad, Margaret Sharkey was a character. He said she was sitting in her hallway talking on the phone. Dad opened her screen door and her storm door. She raised her finger to indicate just a minute. But Dad told her he couldn't wait because the baby was coming. Mrs. Sharkey never said goodbye to the person to whom she was speaking. She just hung up the phone and ran after Dad. The houses were very close togeth-er. They ran through the yards. When they came through the front door, Thad was standing there and looked up at her. Mrs. Sharkey was wearing nothing but a duster. She had just gotten out of bed after working a night shift. Thad looked up at her and asked if she was a witch. My father laughed as he recounted that part of the story.

Dad and Mrs. Sharkey ran to the bedroom. Dad admitted he didn't know what to do under the circumstances. Mrs. Shar-key instructed him to get some clean towels. Then she and my father tried to keep the baby from coming too quickly. Mrs. Sharkey was concerned about the cord being wrapped around the baby's neck. Although my mother was enduring an unmed-icated childbirth, Dad claims she was trying to console him. She said his eyes were huge, and she feared he might have a heart attack. But moments later, the baby was there, and Mom was happy. She was lying on the bed and asked for the baby. Dad and Mrs. Sharkey handed her to mom. She held the baby in front of her and welcomed her into the family. By then, Grandpa was there. The baby arrived before Grandpa did.

Dad tried to call the fire department to get an ambulance. His hands were shaking so badly that Grandpa had to dial the rotary phone. Dad said the ambulance got there pretty fast. The paramedics came in the door with a stretcher. They turned it up on its' end to get it back to the bedroom. The paramedics wanted to cut the umbilical cord. But Mom had the presence of mind to tell them they shouldn't cut the cord because she hadn't passed the afterbirth yet. Dad called the doctor's office and confirmed that Mom was right. They recommended trans-porting Mom to the hospital with the baby on her stomach since she hadn't passed the afterbirth. The paramedics acqui-esced and put Mom on the stretcher. She held the baby as they took her out the front door. All the kids were outside. Mom yelled to everyone, "It's a girl, it's a girl."

The old St. Elizabeth North Hospital wasn't far from our house on Ashland Avenue. Mom, Dad, and baby Sara were taken to the emergency room, which had little cubicles with white curtains. Mom's obstetrician, Dr. Robert O'Connor, was not there. She was seen by an intern and a foreign house doctor. The house doctor told the nurse to get Dad out of there. Not wanting to cause an issue, Dad went around the other side of the curtain. As Dad recalls, Mom asked to see the afterbirth. The house doctor told her they don't show patients the afterbirth. But Mom was insistent. Mom's obstetrician missed everything. Dad said he looked disappointed when he arrived. At that point, there was nothing for him to do but offer his congratulations.

Unfortunately, the hospital didn't have a bed for my mother. They couldn't put the baby in the obstetrics department because the delivery wasn't sterile. They had to put the baby in pediatrics and Mom on another floor. She was on a stretcher out in the hall. Dad was the attorney for St. Elizabeth Hospital at the time. Sister Cornado was the administrator. She saw Dad standing beside my mother in the hall and asked what had happened. My parents explained that my mother had given birth at home under primitive conditions, and the hospital didn't have a bed for her.

Sister Cornado intervened and somehow found my mother a bed in a semi-private room. Her roommate's name was Mattie Miller. She had surgery on her back and had been there for several weeks. According to Dad, Mattie Miller was glad to share her room with Mom. Having a young roommate was a nice change for her.

Dad stayed at the hospital for a little while before heading back to the office to lock up. Then he stopped at Frisch's and bought three Big Boys and a pumpkin pie for Mom, Mattie Miller, and himself. Dad returned to the hospital, and the three of them had dinner together.

~

Eventually, our family moved from Ashland Avenue to the country in Independence, Kentucky. My father bought the

Green Road farm at an estate auction. They were selling the property in three pieces. The night before the auction, my father drove out to the property with Judge Benzinger. After looking at the farm, Judge Benzinger recommended they buy it.

The land had a rich history which my father told me in detail. George Kaub came to the United States from Germany in the 1870s and accumulated 600 acres of property. He raised sheep. George Kaub died in 1927, leaving behind two daughters and a son. Kaub's oldest daughter was Mamie Fahey. Mamie Fahey inherited about 240 acres as a life estate in the farm. Upon her death, the land went to her children, Kaub's grandchildren. Mamie Fahey died in 1958. My father purchased the Green Road farm from her estate auction.

Some of Mamie Fahey's children had died and left minor children. Consequently, they land had to be sold under court direction to protect the minors' interests. The estate sale was considered a Master Commissioner sale because there were minor heirs.

George Kaub's second daughter was Gertrude Blau. Her husband, Nick Blau, had been married before. His first wife had died. Nick Blau and his first wife had two children together. Gertrude and Nick Blau had one child together; Nick Jr. George Kaub left 150 acres to his daughter, Gertrude Blau, as a life estate in the farm. Kaub specified that the land should be inherited by Gertrude's "children of the blood". Upon her death, Nick Jr. was the sole heir of her land. Upon Nick's death, the farm would be inherited by his other grandchildren. George Kaub made this provision because Nick was in the seminary, and Kaub didn't think Nick would ever have children.

George Kaub left the remaining two hundred acres of the farm to his son, George. This was 200 acres. George was a successful farmer with a large family. He built a big dairy barn in 1930, right in the middle of the depression.

After buying the Green Road farm from the estate auction in 1958, Judge Benzinger and my father named the farm Ben-D.

Judge Benzinger unexpectedly died on Christmas Eve in 1960. After he died, the Judge's wife, Elfreda, wanted to sell her interest in the farm. Their only child, Gerald, was only sixteen when his father died. Gerald would later become my father's law partner. My father bought Elfreda's interest in the farm. Although my father and the Judge only owned the farm together for a short time, my father still uses the name Ben-D for the farm today.

Initially, my parents planned for the farm on Green Road to be a summer home while we continued living downtown. My father looked at a lot across the street from Holy Cross School because he thought of having to haul all of us children to school every morning. My father laughs as he recalls he had eleven children in seven schools at one time. When my father was trying to buy the lot across the street from the Holy Cross School, Amy was in the second or third grade and was attending Villa Madonna Academy. My father recalls her coming home and telling him and my mother what girls at school were telling her about life. That's when my parents decided they should move the family to the Green Road farm. They believed they would have more control and influence over us because there was no one else around to influence us. My parents also thought moving to the farm would help with academics.

So, in 1965 we moved to the country. My parents had eight children then, but three more would be born on Green Road. Celia was just a baby when we moved. Richard was the first child born after we moved to the farm. When we moved to Green Road, Mom recalls asking Dad if he would start coming home for dinner because his kids never got to see him. Dad began coming home for dinner before heading back out for meetings in the evening.

My first recollection of our move to Green Road involves a faded memory of riding in the back of a black, flatbed GMC dump truck. This memory is my first memory, period. I was only two years old. Green Road was a curvy gravel road that stretched about five miles between what was known as Walton-Nicholson Road or Rt. 16 and U.S. 25 or Dixie Highway.

Green Road traversed Kenton County between two towns; Independence and Walton. My formative years from two to twenty-four involved life on Green Road.

When my father bought the farm, Green Road was a gravel road, and we had a gravel driveway. Dad planted Pin Oak trees alongside the driveway, which are now about two feet in diameter and a hundred feet tall. When we moved to the Green Road farm, my father had to put an addition on to the house. Over the years, my parents added on to our home three or four times, creating a sprawling house. My father added what he called a dormitory where he housed five of us boys. The dormitory was a big, two-story-like barn. Each corner had a single bed, footlocker, dresser, closet, and window. We each had a desk with a light hanging above it so it wouldn't bother anyone else when we were studying. We also had a bookshelf above our beds. The ceiling in the dormitory was so tall we could string ropes from the rafters and play Tarzan from our beds. We also drew chalk marks above the doors where we could play full-court basketball. There was a bathroom off our big room for us to use. In the bathroom, we had a urinal. There were four boys at the time: Thad, Jed, Seth, and me.

Dad recalls speaking to the salesman when he and Mom purchased the furniture for the dormitory. The salesman pondered aloud whether my parents might have more boys in the future. Consequently, my parents ended up buying beds that could be bunk beds. Although they only had four boys at the time, they purchased six beds, and made one a bunk bed. Thad later slept over Richard. However, my parents later added more rooms, and we didn't need the bunkbeds anymore.

As kids growing up on Green Road, my mother completely restricted our television watching. Mom thought cartoons were too violent, so we were not allowed to watch Saturday morning cartoons. But it really didn't matter because we were too busy working on the farm to watch them anyway. We were restricted to watching *Little House on the Prairie*, the *Waltons*, the *Disney* Sunday night movie, Tarzan movies,

John Wayne movies, and sporting events. We loved all the Tarzan movies. Tarzan, Jane, Boy, Cheetah the Chimpanzee, the Dambuddies, the quicksand, the elephant stampedes, all of it. However, our favorite episode was when Tarzan went to New York City. It's a classic. In many ways, Seth is Tarzan in New York City every day.

Lent was a special occasion for my mother to inflict punishment upon us from the Good Lord. She would restrict us from watching any television for forty days. Although there were only four channels at the time, this was hell. Mom would tie a purple bow around our one television in a manner that she would know if we ever untied it. Those forty days always went by so slowly.

Being from a strict Catholic family, my mother and father made us say the rosary after dinner every May and every October. This made us uncomfortable when we had a friend over for dinner. We had to explain that they needed to sneak out and play basketball alone for thirty minutes, or say the rosary with us.

When friends came over to our house on Green Road, they would marvel at the length of our kitchen table. Our kitchen table was long enough to seat more than our thirteen family members. Since there were thirteen of us, my parents always had a station wagon. Today large families need an SUV or minivan that might seat seven or eight people. But back then, large families like ours drove station wagons. To this day, I still don't understand how all thirteen of us fit in a station wagon. But every Sunday, we all climbed in the station wagon and went to church together at St. Cecelia's Catholic Church. St. Cecelia's always held a Labor Day Festival the first week in September. This is your typical festival which every church in America holds once a year to help finance whatever the church needs. They had bingo, games, meals in the cafeteria, and hayrides. I recall trying to make $5 last all day with my friend, Donald Osborne. When we got down to our last dime, we would try one desperate chance at bingo. Sometimes we were successful.

Aside from the challenges of transporting such a large family, feeding such a large family is also challenging. For breakfast, there were boxes and boxes of Kellogg's cereal. Sometimes we ate toast. Sometimes my mother would cook eggs. I recall requesting pancakes once a week, which she always made for me. My mother usually cooked our dinners in a pot. There would be a pot of chili, a pot of stew, a pot of soup, anything that would work with a pot. We also enjoyed hamburgers, hot dogs, meatloaf, mashed potatoes, and the general American fare midwestern families eat. Sitting across from my brothers and racing to eat our mashed potatoes the fastest was always fun. Whoever finished first got the last batch left in the pot. We would act like we weren't watching to see how fast the others were eating, but secretly, we kept a close eye on each other. My dad took us out to eat at least once a week, usually after church. Our favorite places to go were Frisch's or the Dairy Queen in Walton. I don't know how many times all thirteen of us would put on our pajamas and go to the Dairy Queen to eat. It was the highlight of our day.

My sister, Sara, and I grew up with the insecurity complex that the four oldest, Amy, Suzy, Thad, and Jed always got to do special things. One of these things was a cross-country road trip to Cheyenne, Wyoming, to see a rodeo. Sara and I were left behind with Granny. While they were gone, I mowed the grass with the riding lawn mower for the first time. It was great fun until I drove the lawnmower into a tree and broke it.

There were a few drawbacks to our house on Green Road. At some point, my father thought he could heat our entire house with firewood. We had four firewood stoves out in the garage. So, we would cut enough and burn enough firewood to keep four stoves burning 24/7. Still, the house was so cold during the wintertime. Even if we stoked the fire all night long, we had to sleep under about four blankets and always woke up with ice on our foreheads. At least, that's how it seemed. Later, I think my dad realized that the expense of cutting, housing, and hauling the firewood wasn't worth it, and he stopped doing it.

When you live on a rural road, Halloween is a challenge. So, my parents dressed us in our costumes and drove us around to their friends' houses to get our trick or treats. Repeatedly getting in and out of the car in our costumes was a pain. Then the next day at school, we would hear from our friends that they collected twenty times more candy than we did by going to subdivisions, door to door.

Growing up on a rural road without city water is a disaster. We had to rely upon rainwater collected from the rooftops and hauling water. My Dad had Jimmy Warren weld a square metal tank that he could slide in the back of one of our dump trucks so we could haul water to fill up our cisterns when we ran out. The number of times we ran out of water when one of my sisters was in the middle of a shower was countless. I remember my sister, Amy, once running downstairs fully lathered with soap, towel wrapped around her, so mad that we had run out of water. She walked down to a metal swimming pool and jumped in to lather off. One of the worst jobs in the world was when we had to clean the cistern, which meant pumping out the water left in the bottom and then using bleach, which would make your eyes burn. To make matters worse, we always found a dead squirrel, chipmunk, or snake when we cleaned out the cistern. Recently, when I had the misfortune of tasting cistern water again, I could not believe that we drank, cooked, and washed with cistern water all those years.

Living on the farm, we were also isolated from the rest of the world, escaping only to go to school, church, the grocery store, and occasionally to get haircuts. Our whole world was on Green Road. The only kids we could play with were the Bachs who lived down the street. Unfortunately, only one of them cared about sports. I remember playing baseball, basketball, and football one-on-one with Jerry Bach.

In 1968, a few years after we moved to the farm on Green Road, my father also bought the East Bend farm along the Ohio River in Boone County. In 1975, he sold that farm to Duke

Energy. With that money, he purchased a sixty-acre farm at the end of Green Road and a hundred-acre farm in Boone County.

~

James Dressman defeated Judge Wehrman in the election for county judge of Kenton County. That election marked the beginning of a lifelong relationship between Judge Dressman and my father, Charlie Deters. My grandfather, who was editor of the *Kentucky Time Star*, asked Judge Dressman to give my father a job when he graduated from law school. Dad jokes that he thought Judge Dressman hired him because he was a fine, young prospect, not realizing it was a political favor. My father joined William Dunn and James Dressman at the law firm; Dressman, Dunn, and Deters. After being elected to county judge, James Dressman was not a partner, but he maintained an office with my father throughout his legal career until his death. William Dunn was elected as a district judge, then a circuit judge in Kenton County, and was even later elected to the Kentucky Court of Appeals.

Judge Dressman was a frank, straight-talking lawyer in the mode of Harry Truman. He was definitely a yellow dog Democrat. Bill Dunn was a huge man who had a bawdy sense of humor. He was not afraid to tell a racist, sexist, or off-color joke, even in the presence of women. On the contrary, he enjoyed doing so. When the Chamber of Commerce honored Judge Dressman after he retired from the Kenton County Fiscal Court out of regalia, he told the audience that Dressman, Dunn, and Deters ended when he and Judge Dunn became judges and Charlie Deters went into money.

My father had other law partners, including Doug Stephens, before he became the Kenton Circuit judge and Larry Grause. He later opened the Conservatory Nightclub and the Glass Menagerie. There were other lawyers that either law clerked or had offices in the Deters law firm over the years as well. This group included Lanny Holbrook, Wayne Bidges,

Dick Nelson, Frank Wichmann, Judge Wichmann, Bill Robinson, and many others.

The firm eventually became Deters, Benzinger & LaVelle. Over many years, Deters, Benzinger, & LaVelle grew to be the largest law firm based in Northern Kentucky before my father retired. The firm grew because my father represented the Diocese of Covington, beginning with Bishop Ackerman, and the Diocese ran St. Elizabeth Medical Center.

Aside from the law, my father had many other skills and interests. His favorite thing to do in the world is to operate a bulldozer. My dad has used the bulldozer on the farm to clear trees, for grading, and to open the road following a snowstorm. Greater Cincinnati and Northern Kentucky were hit by a blizzard in 1978. The snowdrifts were about 10-foot-high. My father drove his bulldozer from one end of the road to the other and opened it up. He said he felt like John Wayne.

The Kenton County Fair has always hosted tractor pulls. In the 1970s, it was a big deal. Charlie had lots of tractors. In fact, he had the two largest tractors in Southern Kenton County. His big tractor, a Massey Ferguson 1100, would spot the drag for the tractor pull. His other tractor, the 180 Massey Ferguson, actually won the tractor pull two times.

I once entered the Kenton County tractor pull light-weight division with a 135 Massey Ferguson. I made a tactical mistake and did not spot the drag. Consequently, I was the first tractor to be out of the running, and I was humiliated.

My father raised Black Angus cattle. At one point, he had about three hundred requiring constant attention. We had to chase them to the corral at the back of the farm. I always thought it was cool that we had a corral. The cattle needed to be fed hay and silage in the wintertime. When the young calves gave birth, we performed the daily ritual to make them steers.

Sometime in the 1970s, my father met Herb Stephens and decided to get into the racehorse business. Previously, William Dunn and Judge Dressman had purchased some racehorses with Bob Hoffman under the name No Dough Stables. I'll never forget hearing about *Hasty Hop Light*, a racehorse that showed great promise. According to legend, *Hasty Hop Light's* tail got caught in the starting gate and killed her as she took off at the start of a race.

No Dough Stables were the owners of a horse named *Quick & Wise*. *Quick & Wise* lived 20 years. My Dad made sure she had a proper burial on the farm when she died. I will never forget that.

The first horse Charlie bought on his own through Herb Stephens was *Palette*. My father purchased *Palette* at an auction. She was a great broodmare and made my father a lot of money. The second horse that he bought was named *Consanguineous*. She also proved to be a solid broodmare.

Over the years, my father has bought, sold, and bred racehorses, including some stakes winners and some good, quality breeders. The best horse my father ever owned was *Down the Aisle*. She raced in the Breeder's Cup and won over a million dollars.

My father built horse barns on our farm and had a full-fledged horse operation. We used to joke that the horses were better cared for than us kids because of how they were treated. We always wondered why Dad spent so much money on the horses, but we drove used cars.

As Dad started building the horse farm, it included building miles of board fence. My brother Jed and I painted the first section of board fence. I remember being on one side of the fence with my brush while Jed was on the other side with his brush. We listened to WSAI on the radio while we painted. Painting twenty sections of fence took us all day. We kept track of our records. Jed and I got so much white paint on ourselves that our blue jeans could stand up in the corner of our room and be jumped in the next morning. We also painted many boards before they were placed on the fence posts. On rainy days we would paint fence boards in the barns. Eventually, Dad decided it might be a good idea to buy a paint sprayer. Now all the fence gets painted with a paint sprayer.

Every year at the Kentucky Derby, beginning with *Secretariat's* race, which I think was in 1971, my father hosted a derby party. At the derby party, they ran a book, and they also drew names. Dad hired bartenders with a full bar and served Mint Juleps. He cooked his homegrown roast beef, which he sliced for his guests. Dad also served my Aunt Jan's potato salad and showed off his horses through a parade for his guests.

My father also decided to build a grape arbor. I guess he was going to become a winemaker too. Dad asked me to help him build it on a rainy fall Sunday when the Cincinnati Bengals were playing. At the time, I was ten or eleven and not very happy about missing the Bengals game. Consequently, I was showing attitude as I held the boards for my father as he nailed them to the post. I'll never forget this day as long as I live. My father told me very clearly, you better straighten up, stop the attitude, and you better not drop the board. As soon as he said this, the wet board slipped out of my hand and fell to the ground. His response was immediate and swift. Dad took the handle of his fiberglass hammer and whacked me on top of the head. I saw stars and almost passed out. However, I didn't drop any more boards for the rest of the day.

～

When one thinks of the 1960s, the Civil Rights movement, hippies, Woodstock, protests, riots, the Cold War, Vietnam, the assassination of JFK, RFK, and Martin Luther King, JR., and general social upheaval comes to mind. I was born in 1963 and was only four months old when JFK was shot. I imagine my parents, with their growing brood, looking at us in our beds at night, wondering what kind of world they were bringing us into.

Seth Riley Deters was born on September 16, 1964. When my parents brought their newborn son, Seth, home to our house on Ashland Avenue, they never noticed anything wrong with him. But as time passed, and after seeing the newborn picture taken at the hospital, my parents realized something was awry.

Dr. Robert O'Connor delivered Seth at St. Elizabeth Hospital. My father was on the Hospital Board at that time. In 1964, the nurses were on strike, and turmoil surrounded the hospital. Seth was born in the middle of the nurse's strike.

My parents regarded Dr. O'Connor, now deceased, as a wonderful obstetrician. His wife, Marge, attended mass every day like my mother. Their son, Brian, was a senior at Covington Latin School when I was a freshman. He was assigned to be my "big brother." I'm not sure how tall Brian is, but I'd guess he's six foot six or six foot eight. Brian was a great basketball player. The New York Knicks drafted him out of little Thomas More College in Northern Kentucky.

As my mother recalls, when she delivered Seth, Dr. O'Connor asked her if she needed anything for pain. She said no and just took a couple Tylenol before she left home. The whole family was happy about Seth's arrival. Mom proudly expresses that Seth was a beautiful little baby. My father recalls nothing abnormal about Seth's birth. The first thing he noticed was that Seth didn't raise his head very much. Seth was about six months old when my mother noticed our neighbor's baby boy, who was the same age, could sit up much straighter than Seth. My mother claims the rest of us sat up early and walked early.

Mom took Seth to see Dr. Tom Egan and Dr. William Temple. As soon as she put Seth on the exam table, Dr. Egan went out and got Dr. Temple. They told my mother something was wrong with Seth. First, they referred Seth to Dr. Richard Menke, an orthopedic, friend and high school classmate of my father. Dr. Menke looked at Seth and predicted he would eventually walk and advance. However, he said Seth would never have a normal gait but "would have a swag to him."

The next medical stop was Dr. Robert Dignan at Children's Hospital. My mother recalls Dr. Dignan was from New Zealand and had a heavy accent. However, my father believes he was from England. Dr. Dignan confirmed the diagnosis of cerebral palsy. Like my mother noticed in Seth, infants with cerebral palsy are slow to develop motor skills like rolling over, sitting, crawling, smiling, or walking. Cerebral palsy can develop in utero or after birth.

Cerebral palsy is not a disease that's transferred. Cerebral refers to the brain, and palsy means weakness or problems with the muscles. Effects of cerebral palsy include involuntary movements, speech impairment, reduced motor skills, and learning disabilities. Seth suffers from all of these. Gratefully, he is not cursed with other symptoms of cerebral palsy, which afflict so many such as seizures, bladder and bowel control issues, muscle spasticity, difficulties in feeding or swallowing, visual impairment or abnormal visual sensation and perception. Seth has never had surgery, and he doesn't have chronic or congenital pain. Although Seth did drool as a youngster, this improved as he matured. Seth can care for himself despite his cerebral palsy. He bathes and dresses on his own. Seth can fix himself a sandwich or simple meal and needs no assistance going to the bathroom. Fortunately, there is no evidence to support a reduced life expectancy for Seth or those like him. However, those with cerebral palsy who are wheelchair-bound and require nursing care could develop health concerns that may reduce life expectancy.

Cerebral palsy was first diagnosed as its current name and condition by an English surgeon named William Little in the 1860s. At that time, the condition bore his name, Little Disease. Sigmund Freund weighed in with this observation: "Difficult birth, in certain cases, is merely a symptom of deeper effects that influence the development of the fetus."

According to the United Cerebral Palsy Foundation, there are 800,000 children and adults in the United States living with one or more of the symptoms of cerebral palsy. The Centers for Disease Control and Prevention estimates that 10,000 babies a year born in the U.S. will develop cerebral palsy.

There are four types of brain damage which cause cerebral palsy symptoms:

1. Damage to the white matter of the brain called periventricular leukomalacia or PVL.
2. Abnormal development of the brain or cerebral dysgenesis.
3. Bleeding in the brain or intracranial hemorrhage.
4. Brain damage caused by the lack of oxygen in the brain (hypoxic-ischemic encephalopathy or intrapartum asphyxia).

The last one is often related to low oxygen levels in babies due to the stress of labor and delivery.

Cerebral Palsy (CP) refers to a group of neurological disorders that either appear in infancy or early childhood that causes permanent damage to one or more parts of the brain. These areas of the brain are responsible for controlling muscle movements. As a result of the permanent injury to the brain, children diagnosed with CP will generally have impairments concerning body movement, muscle coordination, and balance. Common characteristics of CP are tight and stiff muscles or muscles that are too "floppy"; walking with one foot or leg dragging; walking on toes; walking with "scissor-like" steps; or uncontrolled jerking of arms, legs, hands, or feet. Of all cases of CP, 50% of those afflicted will experience cognitive issues.

There are four types of CP defined by the areas of the brain affected as well as the characteristics of the impaired muscle movements. They are Spastic CP, Dyskinetic CP, Ataxic CP, and Mixed CP. Of these, Spastic CP is the most common, accounting for 80-90% of all cases.

Cerebral Palsy has been diagnosed in approximately 1 million people in the United States and approximately 18 million people worldwide. This means that 1 out of every 345 children born in the world has Cerebral Palsy. While 40% of children with CP are born prematurely, the 60% majority are born at full term.

Cerebral Palsy is the result of either abnormal development or injury to specific areas of the brain. The majority of children with CP are considered congenital, meaning they were born with it. A small number are considered acquired, meaning that CP developed after birth. While many causes of CP are unknown, some congenital causes are gene mutations, infections, fevers, or trauma affecting brain development while still in the womb. There are also fetal strokes and damage to the white matter of the brain which are congenital causes. Brain Injuries leading to CP can be caused during pregnancy, birth, or after birth. The most common type of brain injury during childbirth is Hypoxic ischemic encephalopathy (HIE). HIE refers to brain damage from severe lack of oxygen to the brain, which can be caused by "severe maternal low blood pressure, rupture of the uterus, detachment of the placenta, problems involving the umbilical cord, or severe trauma to the head during labor and delivery". The small number of acquired brain damage cases seen in CP includes infections such as meningitis or viral encephalitis, problems with blood flow to the brain, and head injuries from car accidents, falls, or child abuse.

While Cerebral Palsy is the most common lifelong physical disability in the world, it doesn't always cause profound or severe disabilities and for most people it does not affect life expectancy. However, due to the associated disorders which accompany CP, the majority of individuals with the disease will experience some sort of premature aging by the time they reach their 40's. Those with *severe* associated disorders, will have a shorter life expectancy than the general population. While CP does not progress or change through time, the severe disorders can take a toll on a person's body over time causing a decrease in life expectancy. Approximately 75% of people with CP have an additional developmental disability. The following statistics are all associated disorders of the total CP population.

- 75% experience chronic pain
- 50% have an intellectual impairment
- 33% cannot walk

- 33% have hip displacement
- 25% cannot talk
- 20% are tube-fed
- 25% have epilepsy (seizures)
- 25% have a behavior disorder
- 10% have impaired vision
- 7% have autism
- 5% have impaired hearing

Of the associated disorders, feeding problems, seizures, hearing and vision impairment and limited mobility are the most common disabilities that impact life expectancy. However, this depends on how severe the disorder and on the individual person. The general consensus is that no matter how severe CP or the associated disorders are, the earlier that interventions and treatments are provided, the better the quality of life and anticipated life expectancy.

While Cerebral Palsy cannot be cured, there are several treatments recommended to improve quality and longevity of life. Traditional conservative treatments include physical therapy, occupational therapy, recreational therapy, speech and language therapy, medications such as muscle relaxers and even neurotoxin injections such as Botox. Surgeries of bones and/or nerves can also be recommended in cases of severe stiffness and/or spasticity. Assistive or Orthotic devices such as braces, and splints can be used to improve mobility. Complementary and Alternative Therapies, while not FDA approved, have been used to improve outcomes. These include hyperbaric oxygen therapy, electrical stimulation, hippotherapy (also known as equine therapy, which involves riding horses to improve muscle strength, balance and posture), music therapy, aquatic (water) therapy and acupuncture.

More awareness and research is needed to help assist with the treatments of CP. In 2006, Cynthia Frisina, co-founder of Reaching for the Stars (RFTS) and Senior VP of Strategic Partnerships at the Cerebral Palsy Foundation (CPF) and others from the foundation, designated March 25th as National Cerebral Palsy Awareness Day. These two foundations RFTS and CPF merged in 2019 to help strengthen the awareness and focus on not only CP being the most common lifelong disability, but also in the lack of research funding and treatment progress in the United States. Advocacy groups have urged Congress to increase research funding in both the NIH and CDC.

Research funding is desperately needed since in more than 80% of CP cases, the cause is still unknown. Also, the prevalence of children with CP is 3.6 per 1,000 born in the U.S. compared to 1.4 in Australia and 1.6 in Sweden per 1,000 live births. The lower rate in these 2 countries is "due to better management of high-risk pregnancies, improvements in neonatal intensive care, and earlier detection and intervention standards of care that are not being implemented in the U.S."

Currently there is no "standard of care" or "best practice" for treating a person diagnosed with CP. While widely accepted practices based on the belief that an older brain that has had an injury from a stroke can be "rewired" because of neuroplasticity of the brain, there is no current belief or practice that the same is true for an infant's brain, which makes little to no sense.

Advocacy groups are convinced that the reason other countries are decreasing the rate of CP compared to the U.S is due to the lack of support and funding given to CP. During the year of 2020, out of the $52,800,000 CDC budget for disorders, Cerebral Palsy was given $0 dollars.

Advances in science and healthcare have come a long way, but sadly, they have done little to affect Cerebral Palsy as a whole. The advocacy groups are fighting hard each year to change this and therefore improve clinical outcomes, but this is only the beginning of the fight. Since the decrease of CP is already a reality in other countries, the hope is that the U.S. will utilize its resources in order to make these same positive changes for the sake of all of the children and families that are experiencing the challenges of CP each day.

CDC Funded Disorders	U.S. Population	2020 CDC Budget
Fetal Alcohol Syndrome	0.2 – 1.5 per 1,000 children	$11,000,000
Spina Bifida	1 in 2,758	$6,000,000
Autism/ASD	1 in 88 children	$23,100,000
Thalassemia	Fewer than 1,000 cases in U.S.	$2,100,000
Fragile X	1 in 11,000 females	$2,000,000
Hemophilia	1 in 5,000 males	$8,600,000
Cerebral Palsy	1 in 345 children	$0

[information obtained from gogreen4cp.org]

My father believes Seth may have cerebral palsy because he suffered from a staph infection when he was only three or four weeks old. The infection was near his navel and ran about two inches across his stomach. Dr. Temple treated Seth with an antibiotic at that time. However, the doctor was concerned about giving antibiotics to such a young baby. The infection eventually subsided and went away. But my parents later read that a staph infection that gets into the bloodstream can cause cerebral palsy.

While Mom was addressing Seth's diagnosis, she was pregnant with Celia. After my parents were told Seth had cerebral palsy, they took him to a clinic at Children's Hospital, where they assessed children like him. He was examined by a neurologist, an orthopedic, and a psychiatrist. He saw an eye doctor and an ear doctor. All in all, my father believes Seth saw at least ten doctors. A nurse also came to our house to observe Seth, particularly to see him eating because he had a hard time using his jaw. Seth had to drink with a straw to strengthen the muscles in his chin.

After this team of doctors examined Seth, my father recalls meeting with them to receive a report of their findings. When my parents sat down, all the physicians were laughing.

Dr. Dignan led the group and explained their laughter. While they had all made independent reports about Seth, there was one theme or observation that every report contained, which was that Seth was lucky to be born into a large family like ours. They felt he was blessed because of all the interest in his care and predicted he would do well because his brothers and sisters wouldn't give him an inch. Seth was the seventh of eleven. We all battled him around. We didn't give him an inch. Seth didn't get special treatment. We all loved and cared for Seth. But as he was growing up, there was never any coddling. Despite Seth's condition, no one treated him differently. Seth was Seth. Period.

My mother recalls that Seth was very vocal when he was two or three months old. She thought he was so cute when he did his baby talk. According to my parents and my older siblings, Seth was a happy baby and was always smiling. Hence, he was given the nickname Smiley Riley.

Amy was seven when Seth was born. Suzy was six. They always helped take care of the younger kids. When Seth got older, Suzy teased him at the dinner table. Seth would have a lot of food in his mouth. He would ask if he could show her his food. Seth would laugh, and the food would go all over the place.

Ponzer's Restaurant was a local eatery that served hamburgers, chili, and the like. Jed recalled our running contest at Ponzer's Restaurant. While eating our cheeseburgers and chili, we had a contest to see who could make Seth laugh and blow his food out on everyone else. We did the same thing at Gold Star Chili. But at Gold Star, Seth would blow a three-way of chili, spaghetti, and cheese out of his mouth, and it would stick to the wall,

Although Seth was usually smiling and good-natured, Celia recalls Seth having severe night terrors as a young child. When Seth woke up screaming, our father would take him outside. He would hold him and walk around with him until he calmed down.

Loving and caring for Seth, who had special needs, was a silent emotional ordeal for my parents. My father claims that he could not talk about Seth's condition for the first five or six years of Seth's life, especially not in public. Dad would break down when he tried to talk about it. To this day, he still gets emotional when he talks about Seth's condition and all he's been through in his life.

As my parents recall, potty training Seth was an ordeal that wasn't often discussed. Seth wasn't fully potty trained until he was six years old. Amy and Suzy helped take care of Seth. My mother and sisters sometimes lost their patience as Seth grew older and continued to dirty his pants. Although my father had eleven children, he didn't change many diapers. But he claims he never minded changing Seth's diapers. As my father recalls, he would always take Seth to the bathroom and lay him on the counter, kissing his forehead as he changed his pants. Dad pointed out that changing Seth's pants at six years old was no easy feat. However, since he never shamed Seth for dirtying his diapers, Seth always wanted Dad to change them.

My mother shot home films of us when we were kids. However, from the sixties, these home films have no sound. In one of the more "famous" scenes from the films, I am pulling Seth in a red wagon. I must have been three or four, so Seth was two or three. Seth was smiling as I pulled him along. Then suddenly, Seth fell out, face first on the ground. This is all captured on video. The camera stops. In the next scene, I'm pulling Seth in the wagon again with a big band-aid on his face. Poor Seth. He fell so many times on a daily basis.

Another of my mother's old family films shows Seth, Richard, Celia, and me as young children playing basketball on our concrete court at home. I believe I was seven, Seth six, Celia five, and Richard four. Seth sat like a frog with his legs behind him. He was on the concrete, kneeling, crawling, and scooting around on his knees. He displays no sign of any discomfort. Seth is just happy to play basketball with us. In candor, we would alternate taking the ball from him as ball hogs and then giving him the ball to take a shot. As always, we gave Seth no quarter. We were children too.

Seth has "double jointed" hips. He can sit down with his legs behind him, and his butt hits the ground. This position leaves no strain on his legs. It's remarkable. We all would watch in amazement as Seth would sit in that position for hours on the concrete.

As a young boy, Seth crawled everywhere on his hands and knees. He could move as fast as a power walker. Crawling eliminated the risk of falling. Seth developed a rhythm to his crawling. As he moved, he would rotate his head and neck back and forth and would usually talk to himself. We all remember watching Seth as he crawled with his head moving back and forth with a huge smile on his face. It was a marvel to behold; this boy crawling on carpet, grass, or even concrete displaying a face filled with joy as if he didn't have a care in the world. Suzy recalls rubbing Vaseline on his knees to soothe the scrapes. Seth actually developed calluses on his knees from the crawling. From birth to adulthood, Seth painfully progressed through crawling, braces, crutches, and then a helmet.

You may have seen the football players from the 1930s with the brown padded football helmets on film or in photographs. "*Leatherheads,*" the recent George Clooney movie featured them. These helmets provided minimal protection for a player's skull and brains from concussions compared to the helmets worn by players today.

For years, as Seth struggled to walk without losing his balance, he wore a similar black and white padded leather helmet. Photographs reflect the apparatus. He always wore it except when he bathed or slept. However, sometimes he even wore it to bed. Seth wore it to school. He wore it when he played basketball. Seth's helmet greatly reduced his trips to the emergency room.

Metaphorically speaking, we all fall in life, and must pull ourselves back up. Literally, for Seth's whole life, this metaphor has been a harsh reality. From the time Seth struggled to walk in braces as a toddler, Seth fell. He fell on the carpet. He fell on the grass. Seth fell on the blacktop. He fell on the concrete. Seth fell multiple times a day. He fell while alone. He fell while others were nearby. But every single time Seth has fallen, he has gotten back up. In Seth's case, he doesn't simply struggle back to his feet. He does it with anger and defiance in his face and his eyes. His face reflects not only determination but the irritation and frustration of a man who doesn't want to be locked inside the body he lives in. Seth is afflicted with cerebral palsy. He never asked for the condition. Cerebral palsy imprisons him against his will. Many times, Seth expresses his anger verbally or physically. I recall that Seth once swung his crutch at Richard, missed, hit a tree, and broke it. Other times, Seth expresses his anger in silence. Oftentimes, he will yell, "I can't help it," to those nearby.

Year after year, as Seth would fall, he busted his knees, his elbows and even his head. The bruises, the scrapes and the cuts never deterred him from moving forward. Many times, when Seth fell, he would suffer a gash which required a trip to the emergency room for stitches. When Seth first began to crawl, it was really trying for him. He would attempt to pull himself up to stand, but he'd fall forward and cut his chin. Sometimes Seth fell over backwards. Our house had ceramic tile floors, and he would frequently bust the back of his head open on those tile floors. We also had a tall chimney and fireplace with a two-foot-tall brick hearth in the center of our living room. Many times, Seth's head found the corner of the hearth. I recall holding my breath, seeing Seth fall as if in slow motion. Those falls near the hearth are when Seth suffered some of his worst cuts.

Seth had to have stitches many times over the years, and he had lots of scars. After Seth stopped falling so often, Dr. Bill Mersch wanted to excise the scar tissue. Dr. Mersch took Seth into the operating room, made a watermelon plug on the back of his head, and removed the scar tissue. Then he sewed Seth's head back together cosmetically, eliminating this bumpy scar tissue on the back of Seth's head.

Seth signed a medical release for me so that I could obtain his medical records from the doctor and the hospital for the sake of documenting Seth's story. I was eager to do so based upon my personal recollection of Seth falling and being hurt so many times. I didn't receive records from 1964 to 1976 as they were not available. But I recall countless trips to the ER for his falls and hitting his head during his first twelve years of life.

On May 23, 1976, at twelve years old, Seth had an x-ray of his skull ruling out a fracture. I wonder if a CT scan would have found one. On August 11, 1988, I'll just say Seth hurt his privates. The doctor stated in the medical record that this was one of the most unusual cases he had ever seen. Although the story makes me laugh, I'm sure Seth would prefer me to withhold the details.

On April 19, 1990, Seth hurt his right big toe. On January 27, 1991, he got dragged by a horse and got his face scraped up. On June 14, 1992, Seth hurt his privates again. On December 18, 1992, he fell and hurt his left ankle. On June 29, 1993, Seth got a hook stuck in his left hand.

On January 1, 1994, Seth fell on the ice and suffered a fracture in his hand. On November 22, 1996, he severely cut his finger. On July 23, 1997, he was pushed into a wall by a horse, and hit the left side of his head. Seth suffered a 2.5 centimeter laceration on his scalp. On November 21, 1997, he fell and cut his knee which they x-rayed. On July 5, 2001, Seth cut his head and scraped his shoulder. On September 16, 2002, he hurt his right ankle. On October 1, 2002, Seth hurt his right ankle again. On March 24, 2003, he hurt his right thumb. On April 8, 2004, Seth smashed a finger. On December 18, 2006, he hurt his left foot. Seth has difficulty maintaining coordination with his hands. Richard and Celia both recall when Seth almost cut off his finger using a knife to shuck corn. Celia saw the bone.

Although Seth suffered many injuries throughout his life, he has never been sick except for a few sinus infections. He has never missed a day of work due to illness. Seth, from an unknown source, probably television, decided there must be a medicine to help reduce his imbalance when he walked. While our father explained there wasn't a medical remedy, Seth took it upon himself to ask his doctor, Dr. Troy Schumann. To appease Seth and knowing it wouldn't hurt him, Troy gave Seth some Dramamine. I suppose just like most of us, Seth looks for a pill to solve his problems too.

~

Aside from being blessed by a big family who refused to coddle him, Seth was also blessed by our local community, particularly Simon Kenton High School. Simon Kenton High School always cared for Seth and included him in school functions and activities. Seth also benefited greatly from my parents' ability and willingness to send him to schools trained in educating and developing those afflicted with cerebral palsy. There is no medical treatment to improve Seth's condition except the therapy and schooling he received at Redwood School. The following is taken from the Redwood School on Rehabilitation Center's website:

Redwood's Mission

The mission of Redwood Rehabilitation Center is to assist children and adults with disabilities to function to their highest potential within the family and community, by providing educational, therapeutic, and vocational programs and life experiences. Redwood particularly strives to help and advocate for those who have no other opportunities available to them. Redwood offers programs and services to children, adults and families in Northern Kentucky and the Greater Cincinnati area without regard to race, color, or creed.

Philosophy and Vision

Redwood's philosophy and vision is to serve children and adults with disabilities. We serve the whole person, not just the disability. Redwood is a leader, not only in our programs, but also in the uniqueness of and the approach to those programs.

The Redwood story began in 1953 when Al and Dorothy Wood teamed up with Bill and Sue Reden to create a place where people with disabilities could grow into healthy, happy, and productive members of their community. They were Redwood's founders and first volunteers. Their legacy is one of compassion, generosity, and community involvement. Bill Redden was a physician. Al Wood was the county clerk. The Woods and the Redens both had cerebral spastic children that were close in age. The Reddens had a boy, and the Woods had a girl. Dorothy Wood became the director of the school.

A pilot preschool, originally maintained entirely by parents and volunteers, was started in the basement of a church. Years later, the school became known as Redwood, named in honor of its founding families, the Redens and the Woods. As enrollment steadily increased, a new building was purchased to enable the expansion of Redwood's Teen and Adult programs, and Dorothy Wood became Redwood's first executive director.

Under Dorothy Wood's guidance, Redwood gained widespread financial and volunteer support from the community. A fundraising campaign was launched to support construction of a new facility, and Redwood's programs continued to expand to meet the needs of the community. As the agency's ability to serve an increasingly diverse and medically fragile population grew, more and more people came to Redwood.

Gary Heidrich, suffered from cerebral palsy, but his condition was much more severe than Seth's. Gary was blessed with true Saints as parents, C.J. or "Mac" and Mary Heidrich. C.J. "Mac" Heidrich is known for his ability to repair anything from wheelchairs to special seating systems to appliances. Mac volunteered his time and used his talents to help those at Redwood.

From *Kentucky Post*, April 16, 2007:

When his son Gary began attending Redwood Rehabilitation Center as a toddler suffering from cerebral palsy in 1959, C.J. "Mac" Heidrich began looking for a way to get involved.

Since then, Heidrich has done everything from building wheelchair ramps to serving on the board of trustees at the center in Fort Mitchell. His son, now 49, still participates in the school's adult day program.

"I just always enjoyed working with my hands, so I started looking for ways to be involved," Heidrich said.

"The school was helping to take care of my family and could get things done that we needed to do, so I just wanted to give back."

Heidrich is one of two Northern Kentuckians named recipients of 2006 Governor's Awards for Outstanding Volunteer Service.

The other is Elizabeth "Hayley" Franklin, a Carroll County High School student active in myriad volunteer originations.

Announcement of the state award recipients coincides with the observance of National Volunteer Week, which continues through Saturday.

"When we give of ourselves in service to others, both the volunteer and the recipient are empowered and inspired," said Gov. Ernie Fletcher.

"Volunteerism is caring in action and vital to our future as a caring and productive state and nation."

Barbara Howard, Redwood's executive director, nominated Heidrich, one of two people in the state to receive the Lifetime Achievement Award, which honors long-term commitment to volunteerism at a number of levels.

Founded in 1953, Redwood Rehabilitation Center is a nonprofit organization helping children and adults with multiple and severe disabilities achieve independence.

Heidrich joined the school's parent group in 1962. In 1966 he joined the school's board of trustees and has been active on the board ever since. He was recognized as a trustee emeritus in 2006.

Today Heidrich, 74, helps with fund raising, seeking donations and co-chairing the school's BINGO! Fundraising campaign. He volunteers at most of the school's special events and helps in the kitchen every week.

Heidrich co-chairs the school's Facility Management Committee, which handles the updates and repairs of the school's facilities.

Sadly, Gary Heidrich passed away in 2012 at the age of fifty-four. At the time of his death, he had attended Redwood for fifty-two years.

My parents initially enrolled Seth at Redwood at four years of age. Dorothy Wood was eager for Seth to attend because of Grandpa Deters. He became a founding Trustee of Redwood, helping them raise money for the school. However, Redwood would not accept Seth until he was potty trained. Consequently, Seth was six years old before he could attend.

When my parents first applied for Seth's admission to Redwood, they were told he would have to be tagged. Dorothy Wood explained they would need to determine if Seth's biggest issue was physical or mental. Students with greater physical handicaps, attended Redwood. Students with greater mental handicaps attended the affiliated school across the street. Seth was evaluated through a clinic and by a team of doctors at Children's Hospital. These doctors agreed Seth should go to

Redwood due to his physical handicaps. They concluded Seth was educable to about the fourth or fifth grade.

My father took Seth to school every morning and my mother picked him up. At that point, my parents had kids in six different schools. Amy and Suzy attended Villa Madonna Academy at the time. Sara went to grade school there. But Amy and Suzy went all twelve years. Dad would take Amy and Suzy to Villa Madonna Academy then drop Seth off at Redwood.

One day Dad was driving Seth to school up Orphanage Road at 6:00 a.m. when officer Rodney Ballard pulled him over. The officer put Dad through field sobriety tests while Seth was in the backseat screaming "Daddy going to jail!" My brother, Jed, recalled how embarrassed my father was thinking of his clients driving by as he performed the field sobriety test.

My father recalls one morning when he pulled into Redwood's parking lot and Seth opened the door and fell out. Dad had to lock the car up because Seth flipped out and went right under the car. My sister, Suzy, added that Father Hanses had to drive holding onto Seth so he wouldn't fall out. Father Hanses took a special interest in Seth and volunteered to drive him home from school. To protect Seth from a bad habit of opening the car door before the car stopped, Father Hanses would have to drive holding onto him. Patience is not a Deters trait.

When Seth first started at Redwood, my father thought it was a good idea for him to take a toy or something from home to school with him. After just a couple of days, Dorothy Wood met my father and Seth at the door and firmly stated that Seth did not need to be bring toys to school.

Seth was adjusting well, and really liked going to Redwood. The first few weeks, my father walked Seth to the door and opened it for him so he could go in. Since one of Seth's biggest issues was falling, he wore a helmet to school every day. At that point, Seth was in two braces to strengthen his legs from above his knees down to his ankles. He also walked with two crutches. When Seth entered the school building, he would excitedly take off on his crutches and his braces. After a couple of weeks,

Dorothy Wood told my father that she expected Seth to get out of the car and walk to the door himself. This was part of his training. Seth had to learn to do these things independently.

Seth called his crutches his sticks. When he broke one of his crutches, Dorothy Wood suggested not getting another one. My parents heeded her advice and Seth got along quite well with only one crutch. Eventually he quit using the crutch and walked only with the braces. Then gradually Seth was able to stop using the braces.

Dorothy Wood was a formidable presence at Redwood. The Woods had two daughters. Their younger daughter, Cheryl, had no mental deficits but was physically handicapped. Cheryl had difficulty walking and wore braces on her legs.

The Woods attended Holy Cross Church. Al and Dorothy Wood always walked down the long aisle to sit in the front pew. Cheryl would follow behind them, her braces clanking all the way down the aisle. My father recalls a time that Cheryl fell as the Woods were leaving church. Her parents didn't help her, and they told nobody else to help her. My father felt terrible as he watched the incident unfold.

Dad also remembers when the Woods' older daughter got married. Cheryl was the maid of honor. After they put the linen aisle runner down, Cheryl came clanking down the aisle. Everyone worried that she was going to fall. But she didn't. Dad claimed there wasn't a dry eye in the church.

Redwood School provided Seth with physical therapy, occupational therapy, speech therapy, braces, and a general education with life skills. Part of his therapy at Redwood involved a padded skateboard device. Seth would lie on his belly on the board and push and pull himself around with his arms.

When Seth started at Redwood, he couldn't read or write very well. His speech would leave out verbs. But eventually he learned to read. According to my father, as Seth grew older, he read the newspaper nearly every day. Seth's favorite section was the sports page. Although he never learned to write well, Seth can write and sign his name. When it came to math, Mom remembers Seth's teachers at Redwood put numbers in terms of nickels, dimes, pennies, and quarters. She laughs as she recalls Seth came up with the correct answer every time when money was involved.

My mother also recalls that the staff at Redwood were so good with the students. According to Mom, they had discipline and didn't coddle anyone. She remembers Deb Turner was particularly wonderful with the boys at the school. They were taught practical personal hygiene. Mom laughs as she recalls Deb Turner showing them photographs of her baby being born when teaching them about the facts of life. Deb Turner's son is also named Seth, and of all things, is a farmer. When Deb told our Seth that her Seth has cows, sheep and emus, Seth responded by telling her, "I got horses and cows."

No one had greater influence on Seth at Redwood than Deb Turner. Very special people teach special children and Deb is one of those very special people. She has dedicated her entire life to children with disabilities. Deb felt a calling to work with children with disabilities because she had a childhood friend who was blind but very successful academically. Out of 659 students in their graduating high school class, Deb marveled that her friend was in the top five. They were in Girl Scouts together through high school and would visit six to twelve-year-old mentally ill boys at Longview State Hospital in Ohio.

When asked about her calling to work with children with disabilities, Deb explained that normal people know better and have no excuses. She claims to have no patience with normal people, which is why she likes working with the handicapped.

Deb Turner graduated from Cincinnati's Withrow High School in 1971. Every bit of six foot one, she swam, played volleyball, and basketball. Then she attended the University of Cincinnati, majoring in special education with a minor in physical education. Deb worked at the Hamilton County MRDD as an adapted physical educator for the most severe handicapped children at Dyer School. She then went to the

Stepping Stone Center where she served as aquatic director for two years. Deb went back to school to obtain her master's degree before beginning a career at Redwood from 1979 to 1985. Deb was hired as a classroom teacher to work with primarily multi-handicapped kids. She laughs as she points out she was better suited for physical education because she was too loud for the classroom. Deb worked with the adults in the work activity center, but also worked with the school-age pre-adolescent kids who would never connect with the community, or with a typical junior high or high school. Deb worked with six or seven kids in the morning with fine motor skills. In the afternoon, she was a physical education instructor, mainly teaching the children at Redwood how to swim.

Deb's influence on Seth began in the swimming pool. She recalls working with Seth in the pool. Deb claimed Seth couldn't float for anything. His body would just sink. However, she taught him to trust that the water would hold him up. Seth loved to swim. He would just flail away fighting the water.

Deb also began the basketball program at Redwood. Deb had been involved with the Special Olympics and felt the basketball program was something Redwood needed to promote self-esteem for those participating and to promote school spirit and a sense of community as well. Knowing BAWAC (Boone Area Work Adjustment Center) and other work activity centers for the disabled in the area had basketball teams, she thought Redwood's basketball team could compete against them. While many of Redwood's players were in wheelchairs, most of the players from BAWAC and the other work activity centers were not. Determined to make it work, Deb figured the kids in wheelchairs could carry the ball down the court and pass it to somebody. Basketball practice was during school hours. Basketball games were after school and in the evening. Deb had a lot of help in making the basketball program a success, including Lori Lucas Eifert, now a retired Sheriff Deputy and Remke Markets, the local grocery store, who donated uniforms. Redwood even had their own cheerleaders.

Deb Turner felt the basketball program at Redwood was so important because it gave Seth and the other students a chance to belong to something other than their families. Deb expressed that coaching Seth in basketball was a riot. Seth played guard. He played basketball with Danny Parsons who only had one leg due to an accident on a railroad track. Danny was the best player. Seth also played with Salvador Herald, Billy Holloway and Bill Young. Seth always spoke of the two Bills. Bill Young had a look and attitude as cool as James Dean. I remember him being Seth's buddy. When Bill Young could drive, he would come visit Seth and take him out. I liked Bill. Seth also played softball. His position was left field. Seth also ran the 100-meter dash and competed in the softball throw in track and field.

Like basketball, Deb claimed the Special Olympics fostered self-esteem and a spirit of community for those who participated. When you hear the term "Special Olympics," you probably think of disabled children competing athletically. Eunice Kennedy Shriver began the institution "Special Olympics" based upon the belief that people with intellectual disabilities deserved the chance to participate in sports and physical activities. She began Special Olympics with a day camp called Camp Shriver. The First International Special Olympic Games were held at Soldier Field in Chicago on July 20, 1968. A thousand athletes participated. Shriver announced on that day the new national program "Special Olympics." Today, there are over two million participants in 150 counties around the world. The Special Olympics involves 700,000 volunteers, 500,000 coaches and 20,000 competitions in the world. The Special Olympics oath was adopted from the Roman gladiators as they entered the arena, facing life and death: "Let me win. But if I cannot win, let me be brave in the attempt."

Seth began participating in the Special Olympics when he attended Redwood School. He even participated in state events. Deb Turner fondly remembers Seth's participation. She expressed having a great deal of fun with Seth and his teammates in basketball and the Special Olympics. Seth still participates in the Special Olympics today. His events are softball, bowling, and track and field. Over the years, Seth has collected an entire shelf of trophies from the Special Olympics.

Deb Turner shared countless photographs she took of Seth at school functions over the years. Some of Deb's fondest memories of Seth include his legendary tightness with money. Seth would always ask for money from someone else before spending his own. Deb also recalls that even as a young kid attending Redwood, Seth lied about his age. He confessed to Deb that he told some people he was born in 1980.

On February 17, 2008, Seth's basketball team, the Kenton County Hornets, played the Orange Crush. My sister Sara's daughter, Anna, helped out with the team. Seth's team lost, but it wasn't the fault of his teammate Joey Meyers who scored most of the Hornet's points. Seth's designated task was taking the ball out of bounds to Joey Meyers.

The tournament was held at Ryle High School. More than 350 athletes, ages 8-50, competed on 23 teams. The Tournament is called the Special Olympics Regional Basketball Tournaments in Northern Kentucky. Mark Staggs is the program director. He runs the program with the help of volunteers.

While at Redwood, Seth also had the opportunity to appear in a television commercial. United Appeal chose several children from Redwood to run towards a camera. As the cameras shot the children running up a street, no director could have choreographed this better than how it authentically happened.

Seth tells the story in his own words. "Everybody running, I almost catch up with Ronnie. I almost - I almost catch up Ronnie. I was last. I stumbled. I almost hit a camera. I almost fell. I fell on blacktop. Catch my balance. I got up. I run again."

That United Appeal commercial depicted what Seth has been doing his entire life. Falling then getting back up. The United Appeal never edited Seth's fall. The commercial aired on television for several months. Seth's fall and the way he picked himself back up epitomized the United Appeal, the Special Olympics and Redwood's spirit.

Aside from Seth's education at Redwood, my parents also made sure he received a Catholic education like the rest of their children who attended Catholic schools. Blessed Sacrament Church, which was less than a mile from Redwood School, sponsored a religious program for students with cerebral palsy. The class was held every week. My mother recalls how wonderful the people from Blessed Sacrament were with Seth and his classmates. She was so grateful that Seth was able to receive his First Communion and Confirmation through this program.

In Seth's later years at Redwood, the Kenton County School District provided bus transportation from our house on Green Road all the way to Redwood. This was a thirty-minute trip, one way. Seth formed close bonds with the driver, Mary Hook and the aide, Pam Thornton.

Seth attended Redwood for twelve years. When he looks back on his years at Redwood, Seth remembers falling a lot. In his own words, Seth recollects the time he spent at Redwood. "When I'd go eat lunch, I fall down on the steps big time and blood come out of my helmet big time. My teacher take me to the hospital a bunch of times. I remember Mom go there and watch me play basketball against handicapped people. When Granny worked in kitchen, every time when we empty our tray, and she'd make everybody laugh. She give me a dollar every Friday. She told me she won't quit Redwood because I go to school there. I quit there 1985 and Granny got killed same year," Seth says with sadness.

~

Growing up on Green Road, we had a Christmas tradition which involved all eleven of us purchasing a gift for each other and our parents. Before we worked for money, our father bankrolled the gift exchange by giving us each $5 or

$10. He dropped us off at the Latonia Ben Franklin, a five and dime, and in a matter of an hour or two we were all finished. We'd wrap our presents, and before Santa Clause even arrived, there were 143 wrapped presents under the tree! In these stacks of gifts were combs, brushes, gloves, socks, fingernail polish, army men and the like.

The most famous gift ever given in the gift exchange was Seth's gift to our mother. One Christmas, Seth gave her Big Mama Pantyhose! Our mother is and was far from obese. But Mom has a sense of humor and took it in stride. We all laughed until the next Christmas.

Seth, with his innocent soul, still believes in the Tooth Fairy, the Easter Bunny, St. Nick, and Santa Claus. He also likes to hold onto his Halloween and Easter Candy as long as he can. He would gladly keep his Easter candy until Christmas. Seth loved chocolate. Sara remembers Seth hiding his chocolate in his closet so nobody would get it. Mom recalls finding his Halloween candy at Christmas time. Jed laughed as he remembered Sam the cat having her kittens in Seth's closet where she had made a nest in his Easter basket.

Everyone knows a dog is man's best friend. We had lots of dogs growing up on Green Road. When we were kids, our most famous dogs were Mama B, who was a Beagle; Bandit, who was a Husky; and Penny, the neighbor's St. Bernard. Penny was great because she would let you sit on her, lay on her, and she didn't care what you did. Foxy, another one of our farm dogs, came along later.

Foxy belonged to Seth and was a new stray when she arrived on the farm. Foxy was a mixed breed, and she looked like a little red fox. She didn't like to ride on the farm vehicles, but she still went everywhere on the farm. According to my father, Foxy followed Seth every place in the world. In the morning she would talk to all the farmhands, whining and carrying on. When my father went to work in the morning, Foxy nearly twisted out of her skin. If Dad got in Seth's golf cart, she'd grab him by the pants leg. Foxy wouldn't let anyone near Seth's golf cart. She also found Seth's golf cart a nice place to sleep. Any time Seth left the farm, Foxy went into the garage and got on his golf cart. She slept there until he returned.

Jocks at a young age usually worship professional athletes. Good students may admire a teacher. More often than not, we choose to admire someone like us. Seth is no different. Although Seth is not afflicted with blindness, his hero as a young boy was Ronnie Milsap. During the 1970's and 1980's, Ronnie Milsap recorded and sold forty #1 hits. I own his Greatest Hits CD. There isn't a song which doesn't move me. Milsap accomplished all this by overcoming his blindness. My favorite song is "*Pure Love*" with its upbeat music and that great lyric - "99/100th's percent pure love." I don't see how anyone could listen to "*I Wouldn't Have Missed it For The World*" and not tear up. Seeing himself in Milsap I suppose, Seth sent away for a photograph and received an autograph picture which he kept near his bed.

Seth's three favorite movies are *Radio*, *Rainman* and *Forest Gump*. This comes as no surprise to anyone who knows him and seems rather fitting. Seth enjoys watching T.V. Land. One of his favorite programs is *Andy Griffith*. According to Celia, he also enjoyed *Gilmore Girls* and *7th Heaven*. Seth enjoys any show with a cute girl or simple moral message.

Seth is a very picky eater. He'll eat chocolate pudding. However, if you put the pudding in a pie, he won't touch it. Seth's favorite place to eat is Wendy's. Our family owns several Wendy's franchises including one in Independence. This is Seth's second home. He never tires of eating a double cheeseburger with mayonnaise only, Biggie Fry and a Coke. His food of choice at McDonalds is a double cheeseburger as well. The famous Cincinnati chili chains, Gold Star and Skyline, often inflict Seth with a little more than indigestion.

Seth wants to go out every night. Jose, our farmhand, would take Seth out to eat when our parents were out of town. Seth would ask Jose to take him to Gold Star Chili because it was the closest. Jose told Seth he would always be there for him

Seth using his famous snow blower to clean the barn floor.

Seth putting horse feed in the stalls.

Seth sweeping the floors.

Seth spreading straw in the stalls.

Seth on his golf cart.

Seth and Foxy.

The house where Seth lives with his mom, dad, and sister, Celia.

Ben-D Farm. Seth drives from the house (background) down the main driveway to the barns every morning at 6 AM.

The main horse barn.

The pond Seth crashed his golf cart into and almost drowned.

Seth on the left and Eric on the right.

Seth and family for his eighth birthday party.

Seth as a soldier for Halloween.

Seth playing basketball at Redwood.

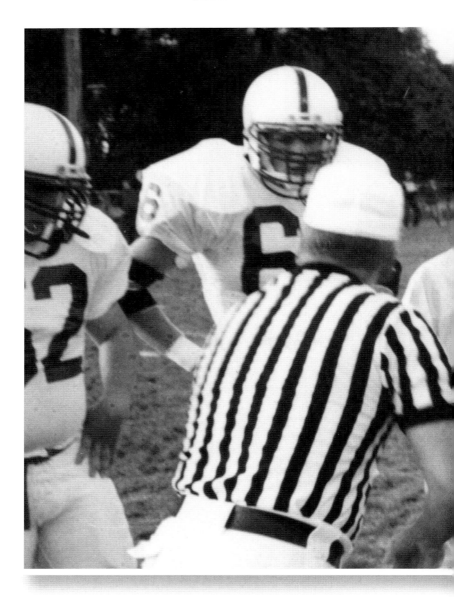

Seth with the Simon Kenton Football Team's coin flip.

Seth at a sporting event with Mary Deters.

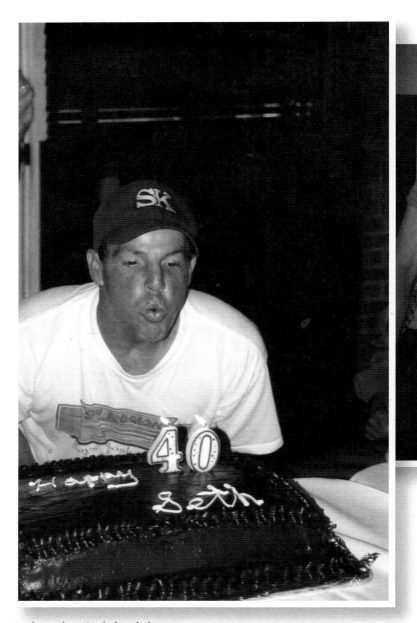

Seth on his 40th birthday.

Deb Turner, his friend and coach with Seth.

Seth shooting basketball for Team Hornets – Special Olympics.

Seth being coached by his niece, Anna Tepe.

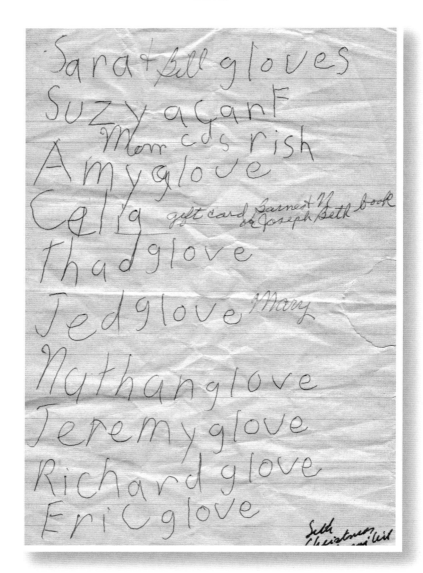

Seth's Christmas list. Every year he maks a list as pictured. It's always the same for everyone ... "glove". Seth makes his own list, and never buys Mary anything or says thank you for taking him anywhere. No one is upset about it. We all just laugh about it. It's very funny.

Seth is named 'Fan of the Year' at Simon Kenton High School, 2007.

so he would not have to contend with an empty stomach while my parents were away.

Our father owned a local bank, Farmers National Bank. Our brother, Jed, was on the Board of Directors. The bank used our father's farm shop where equipment is maintained to store repossessed goods. Deters being self-helpers, Dad once helped repossess a horse trailer in Canada for the bank. He drove all the way there with the President of Farmers National Bank, picked it up and drove it back. Jed was involved in the repossession of a liquor store's inventory. Part of that inventory were porn magazines. The plan was to burn them. But Seth found them before that happened. Jed busted him.

Jed was in the shop working on rehabbing an old truck. He was there at night, like nine p.m., and heard the door open. Seth came in and Jed called to him but got no response. Seth went upstairs and turned on a light. When he came back down, he said goodbye to Jed and was on a dead run back to his golf cart. Jed asked Seth to stop and come over. Seth reluctantly obliged. Jed noticed that magazines sticking out from underneath Seth's shirt. He had four or five of them stuck in his shirt and was taking them home. These porn magazines weren't Playboy. They were specialty porn, the junkiest of the junk porn magazines featuring girls over 40 with big boobs and little butts. According to Jed, they were twisted magazines. He warned Seth that he was going to get into trouble, especially if our mother found out he had them. Jed told him he better find a good hiding place for the magazines or get rid of them. Seth decided he would hide them under the seat of his golf cart. Somehow, our father or somebody found out about it soon after that, and the next day the first task for all the farmhands was to load up all the porn magazines, take them to the dump and burn them.

～

The center of Seth's universe is the farm. The Ben-D farm is quite an operation. Beginning with several hundred acres, the farm grew as our father purchased adjacent farms as they became available. Now the farm is over 1,000 acres.

The Ben-D farm is a working farm. Growing up on the farm, each of us boys took our turn as farmhands. The girls took care of the household chores. In candor, we were paid. I don't know if the girls were paid. We also witnessed the transformation of old wire fence to board fence because we helped build it. We watched the transformation of old barns to new barns because we helped build them. There are over ten barns on Ben-D farm. We have seven tractors and every piece of farm equipment imaginable. We have bulldozers and dump trucks. We raised cows, pigs, and thoroughbred racehorses. There are fluctuating horse counts depending on births and sales. Ben-D farm has an office, a full-time manager, full-time secretary and five to ten farmhands depending on the season. On a yearly basis, they bale 7,000 square bales at Ben-D farm. Everyone, including the "retired" sons help with this cause. There are also 500-800 round bales. We all thank God for the technology of a round baler. There are 275-300 head of Black Angus cattle. These cattle are cared for from birth to death. There is feeding, vets, herding and everything in between.

I have fond memories of chasing cows all day as we would drive them from the fields in the front of the farm, across creeks, down and up hills, through woods to the corral at the back of the farm or to the fields where they would graze. Over the years we utilized our legs, horses and even Jed's motorcycle for these tasks. Back in the day we also harvested our own wheat, oats, straw, corn silage and tobacco. As a young boy, one of my greatest joys was jumping off the corn shed about twenty feet into the soft, sweet smelling fresh cut silage.

Seth recalls when our father purchased a huge blue tricycle to aid him as he traveled around the farm. Unfortunately, there were several problems with the tricycle. Although Seth's legs were plenty strong enough to pedal the tricycle, it was prone to tipping over. In addition, the main entrance to the primary horse barn began with an uphill grade. Coming out of the driveway, it slopes to the road. When going uphill, Seth would sometimes roll back down. When going down, he would lose control and go out in the middle of Green Road running the risk of being struck by a car.

In his own words, Seth recalls the final days of his tricycle. "When I drive the big tricycle, Daddy saw me pedaling. Daddy stopped me. I think Daddy said time to get a golf cart because it's hard to pedal the tricycle."

My father recalls how Seth would walk over to the barn to feed the horses in the morning before he bought him the golf cart. If we had fresh snow, there would be five big steps, a big snow angel where Seth had fallen, five more big steps, and another big snow angel where he had fallen a second time. Seth thought that was funny. But Dad always worried about Seth getting hurt. This was not a baseless concern. Still, my father marvels at Seth's hardheadedness. He can only remember one time when a horse reared up or hit Seth. Recent studies reflect how horses have a special touch with disabled children. My father has seen Seth under horses. He's seen him tangled up in the front legs of mares numerous times. My father has seen Seth fall underneath them. Since Seth has gone into the stalls alone every single day for decades, Dad is amazed that the horses have never stepped on him.

Seth awakens every morning at 6:00 a.m. without the benefit of an alarm clock. He drives his golf cart to the barns. He then feeds and waters each horse. He knows what type of feed and how much to give each horse.

Later, after the horse stalls are cleaned, Seth shakes out the straw bedding and cleans the barn aisles between the two rows of stalls. When shaking out the straw in the stalls, Seth gets the straw in his clothes and shoes. When he comes in the house to take off his clothes, straw falls out everywhere. Celia remembers our mother apologizing to the housekeeper for the mess. For years Seth swept the barn aisles with a broom. Eventually, he talked my father into buying him a mechanical blower. Dad grins as he admits Seth has been through about a dozen blowers at this point. Seth uses extension cords to power these electric blowers. Dad claims Seth has been through 25-30 extension cords because he keeps twisting them as he blows. Eventually he twists them in two. At one time, Dad recalls there was not an extension cord left on the farm.

Seth remembers when he began to work on the farm when he was only fifteen years old. "I go straight out door, and later I get bananas," Seth says. He doesn't eat breakfast. "I go in the feed room. I get the feed cart and I feed the yearlings every morning. Put the cart back. Get another cart, sweet feed, mare feed. Feed every mare. I go down to the breeding shed, feed the mares in the stalls, and feed one of the yearlings down there. Then I go on my golf cart again, go over to Barn Two. Feed the yearlings and put hay and water in. And I always get done the breeding shed, put hay and water in those. I go back Barn One. Put hay and water in, and I put hay and water in Barn One A. Sweep barn and put bedding in stall."

Seth ends his day at 4:30 or 5:00 p.m. He completes his routine seven days a week. Even Christmas is a workday. Seth received training for work while attending Redwood. Redwood had a connection with BAWAC, and Seth took a course on janitorial work. Seth worked in the morning at the Independence Lumber Company cleaning up after mill work, sweeping the floor, and emptying the garbage. Seth recalls working at the lumber company for a couple of years. In his own words he "pick up sticks, sweep the concrete."

Seth made special friends at the lumber company. Frank Armstrong who worked in the mill and Tommy McDaniel who kept Seth busy and amused. Tommy McDaniel religiously stopped at the convenient store and brought Seth doughnuts every morning. Neither Frank nor Tommy works there any longer. Frank began his own business and Tom passed away.

According to Seth, "Tom passed away in Indiana on his wife's lap. He got heart attack. He not here no more. He buy me breakfast every morning up there."

The lumber company, like the farm and the Simon Kenton Community, gave Seth a sense of purpose and provided him with the feeling that he belonged to something. Programs exist today where businesses hire disabled and challenged workers. The benefit is mutual. Businesses receive serious dependable labor. The workers receive the joy of purpose and contribution.

Seth worked part-time at Independence Lumber and part-time at the farm. In the beginning, Seth only worked at the farm in the summertime. Then he worked all year except for December through February. But Seth really didn't like janitorial work. He preferred working on the farm and my father pointed out that working two or three-hour shifts at the lumber company wasn't very convenient anyway. Eventually, Seth became more capable of doing things on the farm and started working full-time.

According to my father, the secret to getting Seth to work on the farm was paying him money. He jokes that Seth never had to be taught accounting. Dad pays him $6.25 an hour. Seth logs his own hours, and Dad believes Seth may cheat a little bit. Apparently, Seth doesn't deduct his lunch from his hours worked, and if Seth is just hanging out on the farm, he claims to be working and charges accordingly. My Dad accepts it, and the farm rolls with it. Seth loves money. Having no bills, he saves everything he makes. However, Seth has a weakness when it comes to donating to the Simon Kenton cheerleaders' car washes.

"I got a bunch of money at Farmers Bank, and I got two CD's," Seth brags. "Not a hundred thousand no more. I took money out." This money was invested in the market. Seth does buy his own lunch and he bought his last golf cart.

Seth has a proclivity for wrecking his golf cart. My father recalls a time when Seth was picking up sawed boards along a fence line as it was built, and disaster struck. Seth was throwing the cut pieces of the board into the back of his golf cart. He missed the back with a board, and it released the brake. The golf cart flew over the hill directly at Jerry Evans and the farm crew. They ran behind a truck. The golf cart hit the truck. The frame of the golf cart was bent. Fortunately, no one was hurt.

My father recalls this was Seth's fourth golf cart. This accident led to Seth's desire for a Gator, which Dad still hasn't volunteered to buy. Celia recalls an incident where Seth was driving his golf cart so recklessly, he lost his bumper. My father states they try to keep Seth off the golf cart at night and they place reflectors all over it for safety.

Jed recalls yet another wreck. He was going to work one morning. The neighbor's mailbox was on the ground and Seth's golf cart was sitting in the neighbor's yard. He wondered where Seth was. Jed drove around and couldn't find him anywhere. As it turned out, a bale of hay or something had fallen off, and made Seth spin the wheel. It broke the steering rod on his golf cart, and he just veered over into the neighbor's yard, running over their steel mailbox. Seth just left it there. Mark Williams came by on his way to the lumber company. Seth flagged him down. He went to work at the lumber company and left his golf cart right there in the yard. Despite the accident and damages, Seth refused to be late for work. Jed laughed, calling it a hit and run.

The golf cart had to be towed up to the Nicholson Service Center. Lenny Collins was looking at the golf cart when one of his cop friends came in. They sent the cop over to the lumber company looking for Seth. He was going to write a report on the hit and run. Seth went out and hid in the warehouse.

Jed remembered yet another crash when Seth first got the golf cart. Our father hosted a political function on Green Road. Seth had been instructed not to use the golf cart because there were so many cars parked on the patio. Jed looked over and saw Seth walking towards the golf cart, which was wedged between Bill Verst's white Cadillac and an oak tree. Seth was walking back and looking at it. He'd get nervous and go back. Seth's face was white as could be. Finally, he had to go tell Dad that he backed into Bill Verst's car. Seth led Dad back to the scene of the crime and told him about it. Fortunately, Bill Verst was nice about it.

Seth once wrecked his golf cart into a tree. The bumper fell off and Jed put it back on. When our father asked him if he wrecked the golf cart, Seth replied, "Just bumper." Celia told Seth that he drives too fast. "I not go too fast. Brake not work," Seth explained.

Seth didn't always maintain control of his golf cart. One time, Seth struck Jed's and Sherrie's van. He backed into it and ruined the sliding door. He also backed into Mom's car. One time Jose, our farmhand, noticed a huge dent in his wife's van. He suspected Seth may have hit the van with his golf cart. When Jose asked Seth about the dent he said, "Your van in way." When Jose explained the van would have to be fixed, Seth offered to pay 50% of the damages.

Seth once wrecked Simon Kenton High School's golf cart. He struck a concrete pylon. Our father made him pay for it. Seth asked Celia, "You take me to Lenny's." Again, Lenny Collins fixed the golf cart.

Seth likes to haul trash out to the incinerator to burn. He also, on occasion, would take blocks of salt which weigh about fifty pounds out to the cattle. Cattle need salt, not just water and grazing. As our father was coming home one day, he saw Seth walking away from the farm toward Walton Nicholson Pike. Dad could tell by Seth's face that something was wrong. He said Seth looked devastated. Dad stopped the car, wound down the window, and asked him what was wrong. When Seth doesn't want to answer, he just stares at you. So, he stared at Dad for a while. Again, Dad asked Seth what was wrong. Seth responded, "I'm going to get Kenny." Kenny lives across the street. Dad asked him why he needed to get Kenny. Seth replied simply, "Golf cart in tree."

Astonished, my father repeated Seth's words "Golf cart in tree."

My father made Seth get in the car and show him the golf cart. As they drove up the road Seth recounted the ordeal. He was going out in the field with a block of salt and some trash. The salt block fell from the seat next to him on to the floor. Seth wanted to pick the block back up. He had to walk around to the passenger side to pick up the salt block. When Seth tried to pick up the salt block, he accidentally dropped it on to the gas pedal. The salt block pushed the accelerator to the floor. The golf cart shot through Mrs. Blau's yard with garbage flying everywhere and continued speeding around the side of her house down to the dam of her lake. The dam was like a ramp. The golf cart shot off the back of the dam, flew through the air, and landed in a tree. The trunk of the tree was about four inches in diameter. The golf cart was literally up in the tree. The tree was bent over with the golf cart about six feet off the ground. My father laughed as he retold the story.

Dad told Seth he would help him get the golf cart out of the tree. He grabbed a chain saw and sawed the tree at the base. The tree came down slowly with the golf cart on top. Then Dad took a chain and pulled the golf cart up on the dam with his pickup truck. The funny thing was there was little damage to the golf cart. Dad recalled the top had a little nick in it, and he thinks the windshield may have been cracked. As soon as Dad got the golf cart out of the tree, Seth jumped in it, stepped on the gas, and away he went with a triumphant expression on his face. According to Dad, it was just magnificent.

Jose recalls a much more serious accident Seth had in his golf cart. Early one November morning, Jose heard an unusual noise. At five a.m., it was still dark. Initially, Jose thought it was one of the cows. He drove his van toward the sound, which was in the direction of one of the farm ponds used to water the horses. When Jose reached the pond, he realized the sound he heard was Seth screaming for help. Jose found Seth and his golf cart in the pond. Seth's head was above water, but he was partially submerged and was underneath the golf cart. Seth was holding on to the golf cart which was the only thing that kept him from going under. The canopy acted like a roll-over bar and kept the golf cart from rolling on top of Seth. If not for the canopy, the golf cart would have smashed Seth and he would have drowned.

Seth must have come down the hill to go across the dam. But he missed the dam, and the golf cart went over into the lake. The golf cart flipped over and caught his legs underneath the roof. Seth's legs were trapped. Fortunately, the water was just up to his chest. But he couldn't move because both his legs were held under by the golf cart.

Jose called my father who drove his truck to the pond. They got a chain and pulled the golf cart off Seth and rescued him from drowning. As soon as they lifted the golf cart up, Seth walked out of the water. He was shivering and shaking from the cold. Dad drove him back to the house and told him to take a hot bath. He marvels at the fact that Seth took a hot bath, got dressed, and went right back to work.

The family tried to ensure Seth's safety when he drove his golf cart by purchasing a light so he could be seen by cars. The concept was to purchase the same light you'd see on a police car or emergency vehicle. Suzy claims she could only buy a green or gold color light because red, blue, white or yellow are reserved for emergency vehicles. She chose green because it's the color of the farm. The green light was then placed on the canopy to the golf cart.

Suzy recalls one night when Celia called the ambulance for our mother. The ambulance came down Green Road at 5:00 in the morning when Seth was leaving for work. The driver saw Seth's light flashing as he traveled over to the horse barn. Assuming it was an emergency vehicle of some type they followed him over to the barn!

Despite Seth's numerous accidents and mishaps in the golf cart, I decided I could teach him how to drive a car. I came to this decision based upon a remarkable man named Jimmy Goetz who was afflicted with cerebral palsy and drove a car. Jimmy was the cousin of a childhood friend, Danny Koch. At one point, Jimmy attended Redwood with Seth. From any objective outward observation, Jimmy's physical limitations exceeded Seth's. His gait clearly appeared more affected than Seth's. However, somehow, Jimmy received his driver's license and drove a car. My logic was simple. If Jimmy Goetz could do this, I believed Seth could too. With Seth being only a year behind me, I felt he was missing out, and believed he would have so much more independence if he was able to drive.

On a summer day when I was eighteen or nineteen, I approached Seth about learning to drive. He accepted the offer for me to teach him. His first and only lesson didn't go very well. At that time, I drove a maroon Cutlass Supreme with bucket seats. I pulled my car out into our driveway and put Seth in the driver's seat. With the motor running, I sat down in the passenger seat. I explained to Seth to put his foot on the brake, and we would put the car in gear. As we completed this series of steps, Seth let his foot off the brake and pressed the gas. However, he put too much pressure on the gas pedal, and we lunged forward. Then Seth slammed his foot on the brake. After a few more failed attempts to move forward smoothly, I suggested we back up. I'm not sure what possessed me to think that was a good idea. After putting the car in reverse, Seth hit the gas and we flew backwards into a crab apple tree. The trunk of the tree stopped the car but busted the bumper, and the low branches scratched up the paint.

After Seth backed into the tree, I ended his driving lesson. Sadly, I realized he could not drive or ever learn to drive. When Seth moves, it is deliberate. His motor skills are too slow, and he can't react in a manner necessary to drive. I felt terrible, but it was just too dangerous. I still marvel that Jimmy Goetz is out there driving. As for my maroon Cutlass Supreme, that sporty car later met its' demise on the railroad tracks after being hit by a train. Thieves left it in the middle of the tracks one Saturday night after stealing it from our driveway.

∽

In his fifty-eight years, Seth has never missed church. He takes it upon himself to ensure he has someone to drive him and pick him up. Mom, Dad, or our sister Celia usually take Seth to church. Saturday night Mass at 5:00 p.m. is his Mass of choice because he hates the idea of not getting up and getting out at 5:00 in the morning on Sunday to do his chores.

Mom recalls walking down the center aisle of church, going into a pew, and sitting beside Seth. When it came time for the Sign of Peace, she would reach over to grab his hand and kiss him on the cheek. But at some point, when they walked in together, Seth went over and sat on the far end of the pew. Although Mom is unsure of how old Seth was at the time, she chalked it up to him entering adolescence. She told Seth that she wouldn't kiss him at the Sign of Peace and would just shake his hand instead. But he wouldn't sit by Mom anymore after that, not because Mom kissed him at the Sign of Peace, but because he wanted to be independent.

Since Seth has family members who attend two churches, he alternates between 5:00 p.m. on Saturdays at St. Cecelia Church in Independence and 5:30 p.m. on Saturdays at All Saints Church in Walton. Seth is very impatient as he waits for his ride to or from church. Suzy recalls that Seth would walk out of church if Mom stopped to talk to someone. If someone came by and asked Seth if he needed a ride, he would accept the lift home from whoever it was without giving it a second thought. Suzy laughs as she remembers one night that Seth was down at the end of the driveway waiting for a ride. He heard somebody was going to a wedding and went down to the end of the driveway and waited for a ride.

Seth has a cell phone with countless contacts recorded in its' memory bank. Never bashful, if your number is there, he will call and ask for a ride to games, bowling, to a restaurant or to the store. I suspect over a hundred different people, probably more, have given Seth a ride to or from someplace. How do you say no? Don't think Seth doesn't play his card! Mom and Dad can always drop him off knowing they won't have to worry about picking him up.

One night at 10:00 p.m., my mother and Celia realized Seth wasn't home. They contemplated calling the police. First, Celia drove to Wendy's, McDonald's, and Snappy Tomato Pizza. When she didn't find Seth at any of the places he frequented, she called the police and reported him missing. Then Celia walked in the dark down to the concession stand. There she found Seth all alone eating a hamburger. When Celia berated him for leaving without telling them where he was going, Seth calmly replied, "I not do anything wrong."

Few individuals are more tight-fisted with their money than Seth. Seth, by virtue of living at home with our parents, has no living expenses. Therefore, he can bankroll his entire paycheck. He only spends money on lunch. Asking Seth to pay his own way if you take him somewhere usually solicits a reluctant response. A crowbar is unable to pry a dollar out of his wallet. Seth has accumulated money in cash, and in stocks because of his savings. He has no intention of spending any of it.

Seth often asks my wife, Mary, to purchase a phone card for his cellphone. Many times, Seth forgets to pay her back the $30.00. He once owed me $50.00 for over six months. When I asked for the money at a festival, Seth became enraged. "I know. I'll pay you," he yelled at me. But really, he knew and didn't want to pay me.

Seth never tips the pizza delivery driver. He often orders his pizza from the Snappy Tomato Pizza in Walton. As an excuse for not tipping, Seth claims, "sometimes they don't understand me well." When Seth eats at a restaurant with waiters and waitresses, he doesn't tip. He doesn't grasp the concept of leaving behind a pecuniary "gift" for a meal he just purchased.

At the time of collection at Church, Seth goes to the bathroom or puts in his loose change rather than part with any greenbacks. If there is a second collection, it really makes him nervous. "I not bring my wallet," is the usual excuse he gives Celia.

Like I've mentioned before, Seth can be very moody. However, there is a surefire way to crack him up and make him laugh. This works, no kidding, 100% of the time. If Seth is in a foul mood, you can look over at him while driving down the road and ask him either of these questions:

"Did you fart?"

"Did you see that girl's boobs?"

His response to either of these questions will be framed in hearty laughter. Any variation of these questions immediately puts Seth in a better mood. Seth even laughs at his own farts. Even when no one else is around, Seth will fart and break out laughing. Jed chuckled as he recalled how Seth would give himself away every single time.

~

Every one of us seven boys suffer from a gradually receding hairline. Seth has probably suffered the most. His hair is nearly gone from front to back. A ridge of hair remains from ear to ear. Yet, Seth refuses to shave his head or accept his baldness. He always wears a ball cap. Seth also uses Rogaine to battle his hair loss. As I mentioned before, Seth's hair loss is a touchy subject. If you want to anger Seth, all you need to do is comment on his hair or the lack thereof. I began shaving my head many years ago to avoid the gradual decline in my front hair follicle line. When I began shaving my head, Seth said, "You give up too easy." Despite my suggestion that he shave his head like I do, Seth holds out for a hair loss cure and keeps wearing his hats.

In public, you will never see Seth without a hat. He always conceals his balding head with a hat. Seth loves hats and owns several. His favorites are his Simon Kenton High School hat or his University of Kentucky hat.

Rogaine is manufactured by Pfizer and claims it enlarges your hair follicles and stimulates hair regrowth. The website states: "That's also why you need to stick with it for at least four months. If you use Rogaine twice a day, every day, you should see results by then, or maybe sooner." Seth bought this pitch. However, we are confident the television commercials influenced him. He doesn't own a computer or surf the net. Seth's closet is full of empty Rogaine bottles.

One day, Celia jokingly told Seth he should think about getting hair implants. Days later, she caught Seth looking through the yellow pages for someone to perform the procedure.

Joe Robinson, who works at a Snappy Tomato Pizza location in Florida, comes to town now and then. Joe once took Seth bowling while he was in town. While they were at the bowling alley, Seth asked: "Joe, you got credit card?" Seth tried to use Joe's credit card to buy the implants!

Keeping Seth's hair trimmed is nearly impossible. Many times, it grows long, and he looks like Robinson Crusoe. My parents have had Sindy Armstrong, who cuts Seth's hair, sneak in so he wouldn't leave the house.

"I know what up to," Seth states in anger when he sees Sindy.

"I want to wear it long. Some people wear hat inside," Seth explains.

Seth carries his hat into church. When Celia tells him he can't wear it, Seth claims he's taking it with him "just in case."

Seth didn't need to shave as a young man. Truthfully, he really doesn't need to shave now except for a few stragglers he grows like Shaggy from *Scooby-Doo*. However, Seth sees shaving as a sign of manhood. Jed shared an amusing story about Seth's mishaps with a razor.

Jed and his wife had a birthday party for their son, Lucien, who was turning five. If you mention the word party, Seth will be there. The party started at 4:00. Seth went to the party right after work. He had horse crap all over him and was dirty and smelly. Jed's wife sent him home to get cleaned up.

Seth rode his golf cart back home. He was back at the party in twenty minutes. His face was cut up and he was bleeding like a stuck hog. Jed asked him what happened. Seth said, "I cut myself shaving, my razor broke."

A week later, Jed went to the barn to get a set of horse clippers to trim the dog. Nobody could find them anywhere. Jed asked Seth if he knew where they are. Seth claimed he had no idea but offered to help look for them. About twenty minutes later, he had them in his golf cart.

When Jed asked what he was doing with them, Seth said, "I try to shave with them when my razor broke." Seth had cut himself to pieces with the horse shearers. He told Jed to keep it secret.

Seth frequently forgets his deodorant. Unfortunately, his body odor can be pretty bad. To cover up the smell, he's known to use Mom's "Red Door" woman's perfume. He puts on so much that Celia once passed out while sitting next to him in church.

Seth's favorite activity is bowling. He can bowl day after day, hour after hour. The first thing Seth will ask a new friend is whether they will take him bowling. My parents are usually the taxi drivers who take Seth to the bowling alley. However, he has an extensive bowling call list. Seth bowls at Florence Bowl in Florence, Kentucky and Super Bowl in Erlanger, Kentucky.

Seth holds the bowling ball with both hands on either side. He bends his back forward and launches the ball down the lane with a loud thump as the ball hits the lane. Seth is not a good bowler. Despite many gutter balls, he refuses lane protectors. He will rarely crack 100 (300 being a perfect score). But the score makes no difference to Seth. He simply loves to bowl. Seth even participates in bowling leagues with his buddies.

~

Independence holds three parades throughout the year. The parades are on Memorial Day, the Fourth of July, and Simon Kenton High School's Homecoming. The parades begin at Summit View Middle/Grade school at the north end of town and travel South on Madison Pike to the Independence Towne Center or the High School. Like the typical parades across America, the Independence parades include bands, politicians, fancy cars, clubs, veterans, and floats.

Seth is always in the parades driving his golf cart. Photos depict how he decorates his golf cart for the parades. Seth usually has a few cute girls riding with him. I once had the privilege of riding with Seth for the 4th of July parade in 2007. On this occasion, his golf cart stalled every time he stopped as the parade progressed. Thankfully, it restarted every time. Seth's two favorite passengers of all time are my daughter, Charlie Ann, and her very cute friend, Carly Becker.

All Saints Church in Walton, Kentucky holds an annual Pig Fest in the middle of summer. The event is always on Seth's social calendar. Our sister, Sara, was working behind a bar in the dining room at the Pig Fest when a guy started talking about someone who was walking around there drunk the night before. According to this guy, the drunk person was stumbling all over the place and fell asleep on the porch steps. Based on his description, Sara immediately knew he was talking about Seth. She explained that her brother has cerebral palsy and always walks that way.

Before the time of paid firemen and tax dollars to finance their operations, the Independence Fire Department operated as a complete volunteer force. The Department's annual fundraiser was called the Firemen's Picnic. It was held on the last Friday and Saturday nights in July on the Kenton County Courthouse grounds adjacent to the Firehouse. There were rides for the kids, gambling games, games of chance, a rock band and dancing, a beer booth, and a fish fry. Everyone in Independence and the surrounding area came out for the picnic and met up with people they may not have seen over the past year. Like at the Pig Fest, Seth was once falsely accused of being a drunk. Jed recalls the year that the police nearly arrested him.

According to Jed, they were serving beer out the wazoo that year at the Fireman's Picnic. Seth wasn't old enough to have beer, but he was hanging out near the beer truck talking to his friends like Don Messingschlager. Every time Seth would go out in the crowd, he'd stumble around because of his condition, not from drinking. Suddenly, three or four cops surrounded him and were getting ready to arrest him because they thought he was drunk. Dad and Kenny, my father's farm manager, had to go over and explain to the police that's just the way Seth walks so they wouldn't haul his butt to jail.

Still, Seth has been known to occasionally drink alcohol. One winter day, the farm crew was stripping tobacco in the stripping room. We had six to seven inches of snow the evening before. On the walk to the stripping room, Seth left the typical tracks expected of his imbalance. There was no pattern, just irregular steps with wide lateral imprints.

When the farmhands stripped tobacco, they always put Seth on the tips. Seth would strip tips and go pow. Jimmy Noland would stand next to him stripping lugs. Joe stripped trash. Because Seth couldn't pull the tips the right way, he smacked Jimmy across the face a thousand times with the stalks.

Jimmy Noland is one of Seth's all-time best buddies on the farm. Jimmy was a big barrel of a young man and was quick to laugh and smile. Jimmy and Seth enjoyed verbally sparring with each other. Jimmy is the one who bestowed upon Seth the nick name of Elmer. There are countless Jimmy and Seth stories. Once, while they were goofing off, Seth lost his temper with Jimmy. Seth throws a stiff-arm haymaker when he gets mad. He swung and caught Jimmy in the jaw and knocked him to the ground.

One winter day while Joe Schmiade and the other farmhands stripped tobacco, they passed around a jar of moonshine, or what they referred to as "hooch". Seth joined Jimmy and the other farmhands for several drinks of hooch this winter day while they stripped tobacco. Each drink noticeably burned its way down his throat. As Seth laughed and smiled, he continued to drink from the jar. Afterward, they decided to go out and Big-Time wrestle which was popular then. Little Seth was taking on Great Big Jimmy. Joe was the referee. There was a cattle round feeder sitting in the back of the yard which Jimmy and Seth decided to use like a ring. Jimmy would grab Seth. Then he'd fall, and Seth would fall on top of him. This went on and on. As Jed recalls, Seth started laughing so hard, he vomited all over Jimmy. But according to Green Road legend,

Seth made perfectly straight steps in the snow when he walked home that day after drinking the hooch. The farmhands claim they never saw him stumble.

~

Brett Ross is a manager at Baker Concrete and an amateur sports nut. In irony, God blessed him and his wife, Anita, with two daughters who are cheerleaders, but no son. Brett attends all his girls' cheer events and then "adopts" young men to cheer on in various sports.

Bruce Taylor, who graduated from Simon Kenton in 1981, works for a local utility. He and Brett coached pee wee football together. They are both outspoken, a trait which makes them some friends, but also makes them some enemies.

Bruce and Brett took Seth under their care years ago. They take him to games. They take him home from games and every place in between. Bruce and Brett cut up with Seth and tease him too. They voice their opinions and complaints about other coaches which Seth parrots as his own thoughts when you talk to him. I've always found that funny.

Seth will say, "They need new coach. Don't play right players."

I'll ask, "Seth, been talking to Brett and Bruce?" Seth just grins in response.

Bruce and Brett are great to Seth. They are among his many guardians and friends. Unfortunately, Seth is very vulnerable to be taken advantage of by girls or women because he likes them so much. He's a typical man. A farmhand once took Seth to a strip bar. The strippers were ex-cheerleaders from Simon Kenton, and they knew Seth. Seth got one of the stripper's name and phone number. Jed recalls when two of these young women came to the house to pick up Seth a few days later. Apparently, they were going to take Seth to the bank to help him cash some checks. Jenny, our housekeeper, and Kenny, our farm manager, stopped them. Otherwise, they would have cleaned Seth out. Seth thought they were interested in him because he was special. I explained, to his chagrin, that some girls like any guy with some money in his pocket.

One of Seth's best friends during and since his days at Redwood is Ronnie Mullins. If anyone mentions Ronnie, we all know who they are talking about. There is only one Ronnie. Ronnie has a disorder which causes him to talk incessantly. While I've never been with Ronnie while he's sleeping, I'd be willing to bet he talks in his sleep. While his endless chatter is amusing initially, before long, it's maddening.

My wife, Mary, had never met Ronnie before. One day, she drove Seth and Ronnie somewhere. When she got home, she walked in the door and said: "My God. Have you ever met Ronnie? He doesn't shut up!"

Now, you need to understand. We all love Ronnie. But we are also honest about his incessant talking in the same manner we are candid about Seth and his idiosyncrasies. But Ronnie's ceaseless chatter is something else. If Ronnie called on the phone, in a matter of seconds he would fire off a bunch of questions in rapid succession. A typical conversation would be: "What's your name? What are you doing? How are you doing? What did you do today? What did you have for supper? How much money do you make? Where are you going tonight?" Rapid fire Jeopardy!

For the sake of documenting Seth's story, I interviewed him about Ronnie. Keep in mind, Ronnie really is his best friend with a disability.

"So is Ronnie your best friend?" I asked.

"He's okay."

"Does Ronnie talk too much?"

"Yeah," Seth answers with a smile.

"Can you think of an example where Ronnie talked too much?"

"I went bowling with Ronnie over at Super Bowl, and people — some people, they were working at Super Bowl when Ronnie not know them. He asks them some questions over and over again," Seth relates with his serious face.

"He talks to them even if he doesn't know them?"

"Yeah."

"And he asks them the same questions over and over?"

"Yeah, every time."

I asked Seth if he thought I should interview Ronnie.

"I don't know. He'd drive you crazy," was Seth's very serious reply.

Our Dad had been driving Seth and Ronnie to the bowling alley for years. Ronnie called one day. He usually called four or five times a day. Dad remembers Seth was talking, then Ronnie asked, "You think your dad will take us?"

"Yes," Seth replied.

The next time Ronnie called he asked, "What time are we going?"

When Dad picked Ronnie up, Seth always sat in the front seat with his bowling ball, while Ronnie sat in the back seat. Seth and Ronnie both had their own bowling balls and shoes because they bowled so often. As soon as Ronnie was in the car, he was talking non-stop and firing away questions. Seth sat in stoic silence. Ten minutes passed, and Ronnie was still on a roll. Then suddenly, as serious as a tax audit, Seth blurts out, "Ronnie, you talk too much." Never has there been a better example of the quiet side kicker to a talker than Seth to Ronnie.

After two or three hours, Dad picked them up and brought them home. When they arrived back at Ronnie's house, he always said "thank you" two or three times. As Dad recalled, nine times out of ten, Ronnie would say, "Maybe my mother will take us next time."

Seth always replied, "Yeah sure." Ronnie's mother never drove them. Seth was aware of this, so he replied with sarcasm.

Suzy recalls the last time she took Seth and Ronnie to the bowling alley. She remembers Seth laughing at Ronnie's constant jibber-jabber. Afterward, Ronnie came back to the house on Green Road and played the piano. Although he never took any lessons, Ronnie has the remarkable ability to play music by ear. He plays the piano, and also plays the organ at the church he attends.

Jed and Richard never took Seth and Ronnie bowling, but they both remember taking them to the movies. As Jed recalled, Ronnie never stopped talking the entire time, and after a while Seth told him he talks too much. Richard claims that we he chauffeured them, he always let Seth handle Ronnie because he couldn't.

Ronnie worked at the Latonia Kroger. Suzy recalls running into Ronnie there. He wanted to tell anyone who would listen that Suzy was related to our father, Charlie Deters. Then he asked these customers, "Do you know Charlie Deters?

Ronnie pointed to Suzy and said, "She's related to him. She's one of his daughters. She's Seth's sister." Then he turned his full attention back to Suzy and said, "Tell Seth to call me."

~

Seth doesn't take many trips or vacations. Once a year he visits our cousins in Louisville. They are the Krippenstapels, our mother's family. Before Seth turned forty, that was basically the extent of his travels. Since Seth had never been anywhere, as the sibling closest to Seth in age, I decided to take him on a trip as a "bonding" experience. I don't remember when the idea came to me. But I had the best of intentions and used his 40th Birthday as an excuse to take him to Vegas. My idea for this trip originally included Seth's buddy, Brett Ross. Unfortunately, Brett couldn't make it due to a work obligation, so it was just Seth and me.

The old cliché "What happens in Vegas stays in Vegas" may be true, but I'm going to violate that rule to share the story of my trip to Las Vegas with Seth in 2004 to celebrate his 40th Birthday. To begin the festivities, I arranged for a surprise birthday party at the family Courthouse Restaurant in Independence, Kentucky. The family, the farmworkers and select friends like Brett Ross and Bruce Taylor were invited. Admittedly, when I staged the surprise, I did not think it through very well. I picked Seth up for the party under the false pretense that we were going to Vegas. When I showed up, Seth came out with his bags packed and carrying his bowling ball. As soon as I saw him, I realized I'd made a mistake. Seth was excited and I knew when he learned we weren't going to Vegas that day, he'd be angry.

I told Seth we needed to stop at the Courthouse to eat. The surprise worked. However, Seth was disappointed that he was attending his surprise party and not leaving for Las Vegas.

He sulked the entire time. Mary had prepared a card and a "ticket" for one free Vegas vacation.

Months later, I delivered on my promise.

Seth packed his clothes and bowling bowl again and Mary took us to the Airport. As soon as Seth got in the car, our adventure began. Seth was wearing a bright, multi-colored, tie-dye bandana. Seth's bandana was loud. Not being pretentious myself, I let it slide. I certainly didn't want to hurt Seth's feelings or make him bare his bald head.

Mary dropped us off at the Delta curbside service outside of the Greater Cincinnati Northern Kentucky Airport to check our baggage. As we approached the Delta Representative, Seth pulled out the "ticket" Mary had prepared and handed it to them. Seth honestly believed that was his ticket to Vegas. I quickly explained Seth's confusion, and the Delta representative seemed to enjoy the humor of the moment.

After checking our bags, we walked to the ticket counter inside. We were greeted by another Delta agent who asked us for a picture ID. I readily complied, but Seth couldn't. He doesn't have a license or ID. Consequently, I began explaining the circumstances. The agent requested his supervisor, and I was able to talk them out of the ID requirement.

Our next stop was the long line through TSA security. As we approached the metal detectors, I asked Seth if he had any metal on him. He told me that he didn't. However, I didn't realize that Seth didn't understand what I meant by metal. As

Seth walked through the metal detectors all the bells, whistles, alarms, and sirens went off and TSA agents came running. They searched Seth and found the huge eight-inch buck knife he uses to cut twine on straw bales. You should have seen the faces of the TSA agents when they saw the knife! I quickly explained that Seth didn't understand what metal was and again spoke my way past the obstacle. Good thing I'm a lawyer I suppose.

Despite the obstacles and mishaps, we were able to board for Seth's first plane ride in plenty of time. During our flight, we experienced turbulence. Seth was scared to death, and it was difficult to explain the issue to him. However, I did the best I could. I should also add that turbulence scares the hell out of me too.

After we landed in Las Vegas we began a long walk down the concourse. Seth's tie-dye bandana was still on his head. As we walked, a very friendly, talkative, and obviously gay man walked alongside us. I suppose he was drawn to Seth's bandana. Seth struck up a conversation with him. Then, out of nowhere, Seth began to laugh out loud. I asked him what was so funny.

Seth replied, "This like Rain Man."

I told Seth I wish he had Dustin Hoffman's gambling skills.

I had made reservations at the Bellagio. Although they keep building bigger and better hotels in Vegas, the Bellagio holds its own with any of them. Inwardly, I marveled and laughed as we walked through the hotel with Seth's bandana. Everyone looked. No one wears tie-dye bandanas at the Bellagio.

After we checked in, I asked Seth what he wanted to do first. However, I didn't really need to ask. Seth wanted to do what everyone wants to do when they go to Vegas. He wanted to go bowling.

Much to my disappointment, the Bellagio does not have a bowling alley. I inquired with the concierge and learned we could bowl at the Gold Coast casino. We hailed a taxi and headed to the bowling alley. For six hours straight, I sat at a table and worked, while Seth bowled, and bowled and bowled. He would fall. Seth's ball found the gutter more often than it found pins. I asked if he wanted a gutter protector, but he refused. I asked Seth what his all-time highest bowling score was. He claimed it was 210. But as I watched him bowl for six hours, he never broke 120. Eventually, Seth laughed and admitted he'd never come close to 200.

Our next adventure was a trip to "*Cheetah's*." Now, some of you may be disappointed in me for taking Seth to a strip club. If so, I apologize. But I figured we were in Vegas, Seth was forty years old, and this would be an experience which would not hurt him. I wasn't taking him to a brothel. I was taking him to see something he had never seen, a beautiful naked woman.

I would guess that trip to Cheetah's was the highlight of Seth's life. I never laughed so loud in my life. As soon as we settled into our seats, a beautiful woman walked over to us. She was foreign with what I guessed was a Caribbean accent. The woman was black and had huge breasts. I explained to Seth she would dance for him for $10.00. Seth pulled out a $50.00. Then another. Then another. A guy tighter than tree bark, had no problem having a dancer, dance again and again and again. At one point, as she leaned over him, I looked over and started to laugh at this sight. Seth looked over at me and started laughing too. Then he couldn't stop laughing. Remember the fart and boobs automatic laugh principle? I proved its veracity once again.

After a couple hours, much to Seth's regret, we left the club to go back to the Bellagio. In the cab, the driver asked what brought us to Sin City. When I told him we were there to celebrate Seth's fortieth birthday, Seth exploded in anger. Although this was a stranger we would never see again, Seth, like most women, resented this revelation of his age. For Seth, age is as sensitive an issue as his hair.

Although Seth was willing to spend hundreds at the strip club, he didn't want to contribute anything to taxi fares. As we rode around Vegas, Seth asked, "If I live here, how do I get to Simon Kenton games, fly?" He then asked me if he could take a TANK bus back and forth between Independence and Vegas. In less than a day, Seth was ready to make Vegas his home.

The next day Seth went bowling again, and I took him to a show at New York, New York. Our final day brought more bowling and a night which scared the hell out of me. At about 9:00 p.m., I went to play blackjack. I told Seth to stay in our hotel room and mentioned I would be back at 10:30. Before we left, Mary warned me not to leave him alone, and I should have listened. When I returned to our room, I noticed a "Do Not Disturb Sign" had been placed on the door. Unable to find my key, I knocked on the door and called for Seth. Although it took a while, Seth finally opened the door. He was standing there in nothing but his purple bikini underwear.

"Seth what the hell is going on?" I asked.

"Nothing," Seth replied with a shrug of his shoulders. This is a pretty typical response from Seth even when there *is* something going on.

"Seth, come on. Why are you in your underwear and why is there a do not disturb sign on the door?" I asked.

"No reason," Seth answered.

I had to use the bathroom. When I walked in, I was horrified to find an unrolled condom on the counter. I was mildly relieved that it was not "used." I picked it up with a washcloth and asked, "What the hell went on here?"

Seth sat down on the bed and told me the story. After I left, Seth left our hotel room and went downstairs. Seth was walking around the Bellagio when a woman of the night spotted him and offered him "help" back to the room. Once they were back in the room, this woman offered him sex. Thankfully, before that happened, she stole Seth's entire $400.00 out of his wallet. Seth claimed she looked for my money too.

"I tried to kick my wallet under bed, but she see it," Seth said. Unfortunately, Seth got rolled in Vegas.

On the trip back home, with Seth broke, I gave him $50.00 to last him until he got to the bank. He took a year to pay me back. I swore Seth to secrecy about what happened in Vegas. He agreed. Then he proceeded to tell everybody in Independence.

When I interviewed Seth about Vegas for this book, I asked him: "Anything you want to say about Vegas?"

He shook his head no. Then added: "If you said girl boobies, we get in trouble. Daddy, Mom find out. It might leak out."

When I explained he already told everybody, he said, "I know. I messed up."

Seth is still waiting to go back to Vegas. I think I'll let someone else take him next time.

~

Simon Kenton High School is at the center of Seth's social world. Although Seth is also loyal to the blue and white of the University of Kentucky, his blue and white loyalty to Simon Kenton High School is unsurpassed. Seth's dedication to Simon Kenton High School has culminated in a grand reciprocity of affection. The Kenton County School District has bestowed great benevolence upon Seth. They have armed him with a pass to attend all Kenton County School athletic events for free. But Seth uses the privilege whether the team is playing at home or away. No matter where he is, he just holds up his Simon Kenton pass and walks on through. Neil Stiegelmeyer, the superintendent, would get calls from other schools and he would tell them just to let him go. Our sister, Suzy, believes Seth probably knows better than to use his Simon Kenton pass at away games. But he's undeterred because he thinks he can get away with it.

Seth attends every boy or girl sporting event, freshman, junior varsity or varsity, volleyball, basketball, baseball, softball, soccer, wrestling, track, and football. Often times, he rides the team bus. Seth travels with the team whenever possible.

This is what Seth has to say about riding with the team: "When I tell Coach Steiner, I say, hey, you got room for me. If he say no, I say okay." Seth accepts his answer and finds another ride.

All the players and cheerleaders know him, speak to him, and tease with him. Parents also know him and give him rides.

This is truly remarkable. It's Cuba Gooding and Radio exponentially.

As Seth points out, he works around his Simon Kenton obligations. "Sometimes I go home 4:30 or 5:00. If football away game, I quit at 4:30. When basketball night, I quit at 5:00. When basketball game away, I quit at 4:00," he explains.

At each homecoming game, Seth buys the cheerleaders each a rose. He also asks them to take him bowling. He stresses "age not matter" and prefers to be a perpetual teenager. Consequently, he disdains any public divulging of his age. In reality, Seth is not a "dirty" fifty-seven-year-old man, but an innocent fifty-seven-year-old teenager. His interest is not sexual, but an innocent crush. Seth doesn't misbehave or say inappropriate things. He's actually a gentleman to these girls.

Just like any teenager, Seth doesn't like anyone to know he's dependent on his parents.

When my parents take Seth to athletic events, he wants them to let him out of the car in the front of the school. Then he walks around the school to the gymnasium or any of the athletic facilities because he doesn't want his friends or anyone else to see his parents bringing him to the game.

Seth prefers our parents don't pick him up after an athletic event and always gets a ride home with somebody instead. Since everybody knows Seth at the games, he's able to talk someone into bringing him home. Seth revels in that. Our father feels that's a way for Seth to demonstrate his independence.

Despite his age, Seth is still beholden to our parents. Dad once told him he was not allowed to go away with the Simon Kenton basketball team on a three-day trip to Ashland, Kentucky. Seth snuck out on the trip.

One of the main fundraisers for the Simon Kenton Cheerleaders are the frequent car washes they hold in the local Kroger grocery store parking lot. The cheerleaders and their parents show up with their buckets, sponges, and soap. They send a few cheerleaders to the top of the lot near the entrance with poster board signs and their lungs to call out to those driving by. Local car owners are expected to make a "donation" if they choose at this "free" car wash. I often wonder if anyone ever stiffs the cheerleaders by taking the wash and ignoring the donation. Seth loves the cheerleaders. The cheerleaders love Seth. Despite not owning a car, Seth doesn't allow this to stop his support of the car wash.

Jose, our farmhand, has witnessed Seth's sudden freedom with his money on several occasions when the Simon Kenton Cheerleaders were involved. Whenever Jose took Seth out to eat on Saturdays or Sundays and they saw the cheerleaders at the car wash, Seth always pulled out a $20 bill and handed it to them. While Seth always uses a coupon to eat at McDonald's or Wendy's, he has no problem with giving the cheerleaders his $20 bills.

When Jose asked Seth why he gave those cheerleaders $20, he answered, "I'm going to have Bobby Cook bring my golf cart tomorrow and let them wash my golf cart."

"So, you're paying up front?" Jose asked.

Seth acknowledged he's paying up front. However, he never has his golf cart brought to the carwash.

At the last home boys' varsity basketball game of the 2006-2007 season, Simon Kenton held a "Fan of Year Contest" at halftime. Five or six students were decked out in capes, with their faces and body parts painted in the school colors of blue and white. They wore blue hair wigs and whatever props they could imagine. Tiffany Ponzer, a young freshman algebra teacher, moderated the event. She called all the contestants to the center of the court. They each ran to half court with excited exuberance.

Brent Bishop, a star fullback for the football team, saw Seth sitting in the front row at the north end of the gym. He grabbed him and pushed him out to join the contestants. Despite his not being a student at the school, Seth was immediately allowed to enter the contest.

Watching all this take place from the stands caused my eyes to well up with tears. Seth was last in the row of contestants. The winner was to be determined by the audience. As Tiffany Ponzer placed her hand over each contestant for audience affirmation, the Simon Kenton student body section ignored each one and began chanting "Seth, Seth, Seth, Seth." By the time she reached Seth at the end of line of contestants, the ovation, cheers, and shouts escalated into pandemonium. The crowd's exultation lifted the roof. I, and several others, were overcome with emotion. It was such a warm and loving acceptance and appreciation for Seth that it was impossible not to be moved.

Seth won the "Fan of the Year." However, it was really the "Fan of the Century." As he was proclaimed the winner, Seth, wearing his Simon Kenton jacket, lifted both fists and arms in the air, with the greatest of joy. It was his night. He was on top of the world.

∾

ABOUT THE AUTHOR

Eric Deters is a retired attorney who once was the #1 viewed law profile in the country on the national law website *martindale.com*. *Cincinnati City Beat* magazine once named him the #1 lawyer and troublemaker in the city. On January 2, 2008, Chuck Martin of the *Cincinnati Enquirer* gave Eric the nickname "Courtroom Bulldog." Since 2010 Eric has managed the litigation of Dr. Abubakar Atiq Durrani on behalf of nearly 600 clients who were victims of Durrani's unnecessary and botched surgeries.

In addition to his legal career, Eric Deters has hosted radio shows, hosts *The Bulldog Show*, is the founder of Bulldog Media and BulldogTV, has business and real estate interests, and is running for Kentucky Governor.

Eric Deters has authored four other books: *Saving Grace, Pioneer Spirit, Willie: Radio's Great American*, and *The Butcher of Pakistan*.

INDEX